IMPLEMENTING SUCCESSFUL
CREDIT CONTROL

This, my first book, is dedicated to my first love, my family, without whose support and understanding it could not have been written.

IMPLEMENTING
SUCCESSFUL
CREDIT CONTROL

Alan Dixie MICM

2000

First published in Great Britain in 1997 by Management Books 2000 Ltd,
Cowcombe House,
Cowcombe Hill,
Chalford,
Gloucestershire GL6 8HP
Tel: 01285-760722. Fax: 01285-760708
E-Mail: MB2000@compuserve.com

Printed and bound in Great Britain by Astron On-Line, Letchworth

British Library Cataloguing in Publication Data is available

ISBN 1-85252-218-6

Foreword

How often have we heard the words "cash flow problems" used as an explanation for a company's failure? "The order book was full, pricing structure accurate and costs under control, but we were just owed too much money and couldn't get the cash in time..."

What we often call cash flow problems may actually mean a lack of effective credit control. Every debt begins its life as an application for credit, however informally; and the debtors' book is little more than an historical account of business accepted for credit by a company.

The primary function of credit control is to ensure that all moneys due on credit are paid within the terms agreed. All too often, it degenerates into simply chasing late payment and enforcing collection procedures. There has been little useful assistance from legislators concerning the problem of late payment; the Forum of Private Business recommended a statutory right to interest on overdue commercial debts, and the CBI's 'prompt payers' code has listed out best practice and identified companies adhering to it. Mr Michael Heseltine, the then-President of the Board of Trade, alluded to possible government measures. But these are only voluntary steps and only the conscientious have answered the call, although – of course – conscientious companies are not usually the problem.

Not unsurprisingly, the onus is on individual companies to ensure they have preventative measures in place; which, more often than not, means effective credit control systems. Part of such a system, and so often overlooked, is the need for sound financial information on the company one is doing business with. This also means knowing about the individuals behind the companies.

Those responsible for credit control in smaller companies should remember that credit checks are not just for major organisations. Nowadays any company, however small, can obtain information on another company's trading and payment performance record for very little cost.

The wise credit controller will also know how to look beyond a company's accounts to the directors behind it, and see if any adverse personal information exists, such as County Court judgements, insolvencies or whether they have been involved in previous companies that have failed.

An alarming fact is that over half of bad debts arise, not from new customers, but from long-standing ones. This clearly highlights the need for companies to develop an effective process which includes the use of up-to-the-minute credit information which can be obtained by subscribing to a business monitoring service. By using current credit information, the credit controller is able to monitor the performance of its existing customers, as well as having the most recent information on new ones.

Interpretation of financial information, the ability to get behind the data to the real picture, is now as much a part of the modern credit controller's job description as is a solid understanding of cash flow management and effective debt collection techniques.

But information is not everything. The modern day credit controller needs a personality with strong powers of persuasion and considerable tact. They also need to be able to walk the fragile tightrope of excuses for non-payment, without upsetting the customers who matter, or damaging further business opportunities.

The successful credit controller would do well to remember that research has shown that nearly half of late payments are unintentional. This suggests that more rigorous credit management could reduce debtor days by as much as half.

Alan Dixie's book provides a comprehensive, first-hand account of the many different scenarios faced by the dedicated credit controller in pursuit of the ever-elusive debt. It is a constructive, easy to read account of the practical steps that can be taken to avoid and reduce the bad debt syndrome.

Introduction

I find this book crammed full of useful information and handy advice for the professional and part time credit controller, both prior to accepting business, and once the debt is on the book. This is an informative, intelligent, witty and easy to understand guide through the pitfalls and rewards of implementing effective credit controls in today's business environment.

Alan Dixie has brought a wealth of personal and practical experience to bear on this helpful edition. I can thoroughly recommend it.

David Coates
Director
Experian (formerly CCN)
May 1997

Contents

Contents

11 Why Do We Need Credit Control?   140

The importance of cash flow. The effects of poor credit control. The costs of financing credit. The effect of credit control on liquidity.

12 Factoring   152

History of factoring. The main services. The process of factoring. The operation of the agreement. The financial cost of factoring. Cost comparison. The law of factoring. Conclusions.

Glossary Of Common Terms And Phrases   168

Bibliography   172

Index   173

1

WHAT IS CREDIT CONTROL?

Credit: a brief history

Credit has probably existed in one form or another since the earliest agricultural society: for it is highly unlikely that man's needs have ever coincided with his ability to pay. Investigation of primitive cultures and research into early civilisations has shown that the first credit transactions probably took the form of a delayed bartering system. For example, a farmer who had just planted a field of vegetables would accept clothing from a neighbour on the understanding that he would pay for the clothes in kind when his harvest came in. There is also early evidence of more organised forms of credit, where the giving and receiving of goods was organised through a central authority.

As the centuries passed, so the credit function became more regulated, although it was slow to evolve. In fact it is not until eleventh century China, during the reign of emperor Shen Tsung, that we find the first government loans recorded to private individuals for the purpose of trade. One hundred years later, however, we find evidence that the first truly complex system of trading on credit has evolved, not in China, but in Europe.

The twelfth century saw the commerce of Western Europe revolving around the great trade fairs. These trade fairs would move

13

from one town to another, staying anything up to six weeks before moving on to the next location. Merchants would travel from fair to fair, buying and selling in many different currencies. During this trade a number of complicated credit arrangements would be made.

As the century progressed, the granting of credit became more adaptable; and by the middle of the century, merchants were operating their businesses based entirely on credit. They would purchase goods from one trader, agreeing to pay for the goods anything up to twelve months later. The merchant would then in turn attend another fair, sell the merchandise, purchase some new goods, and so the cycle would turn again.

The financial costs associated with offering credit at this time were very low. This enabled merchants to offer credit terms far in excess of those we offer today, and helped to develop further the use of credit in commerce. The days of consumer credit were still a long way off.

While the great trade fairs were operating in Europe, the concept of credit had also reached the shores of England. During this period basic commodities such as wool, leather, cloth, corn and wine were all being traded on credit.

As credit developed over the centuries, it became more organised, with clearer objectives for the development of trade. During this period, the costs associated with offering credit increased, causing the period of credit offered to contract. Apart from these changes, the basic principles of credit have remained broadly the same over the centuries.

The most significant change in the role of credit in society did not materialise until the latter half of the twentieth century, with the increased availability of consumer credit. This trend was clearly exposed in the UK during the decade of the 'eighties, when the world of commerce experienced a sharp move towards a 'buy now, pay later' mentality. The boom years of the 'eighties were built upon the foundations of revolving credit, and this was one of two main factors responsible for the feeling of affluence associated with this decade. The other was the release of large quantities of council house stock at discounted prices into the housing market. This led to a sudden and substantial increase in the number of home owners, and sparked a growth in house sales and prices, together with a concomitant boom in home improvements and household goods, the like of which had never been seen before.

The cost of decorating and furnishing these properties fell, to a large extent, on our flexible friends – the credit cards. This uncontrolled increase in credit finally caused the overheating of the economy which was a major factor in the recessional trend that was to follow.

History will look no further than the affluent 'eighties for the cause of the recession that followed immediately in the early 'nineties. However, the seeds of this credit boom were planted sixty years earlier, with the development and implementation of the credit card.

Credit cards originated in the USA in the early 1920s. Individual firms such as oil companies and hotel chains began issuing them to customers for purchases made at company outlets. These early credit cards were really charge cards, where the total balance owed had to be cleared each month. This new form of credit was slow to take off and did not increase by any great extent until after the Second World War.

The first universal credit card that could be used at a variety of establishments was introduced by Diners Club Inc. in 1950. This launch was followed eight years later by American Express. The first bank credit card was launched by the Bank of America in 1959. Originally named the Bank America card, in 1976 it changed its name to the globally recognised Visa.

The past century has seen more important developments in credit than any other period in history. As we move into the new millennium, this trend is likely to continue. With the development of 24-hour telephone banking, and the implementation of debit cards such as Switch and Delta, the need for hard cash is already becoming extinct.

The need for credit

Having looked at the development of credit, we should now take a brief look at the reasons why we need credit, and how it affects our everyday lives? The reason I suggest we take only 'a brief look' is because this is in fact a very complicated subject, beyond the scope of this book. The aim of the next few pages is simply to demonstrate how much we as individuals rely on credit, and why it is such an intricate part of life as we know it.

There is no doubt that the principal function of credit is to increase trade. Without it, countries and individuals would not be able to trade with each other. Common trading markets such as the European Union would cease to exist – as would the stabilisation of commodity prices through arrangements such as GATT. Whether we like it or not, credit is part of our everyday life. But what would life be like without credit?

Imagine that, on waking tomorrow, you stumble downstairs, make breakfast, and collect the paper from its usual place on the doormat. Suddenly, to your horror, you find that parliament has passed a law, with immediate effect, banning all forms of credit. Ignoring the fact that most households in the country would become instantly bankrupt owing to their inability to repay all their outstanding debts, how would this new law affect you?

The first thing to happen would be the cessation of all forms of mass production. Companies such as Ford Motors would no longer be able to manufacture the thousands of cars for which they had not yet secured a buyer. Without credit to finance production it would be commercially impossible for them to carry this level of stock. This would also be true for all other mass-produced items such as washing machines, televisions, videos, hi-fi systems and computers. All these items would have to be made to order. In fact, to be able to finance the manufacture of each item, the company would probably have to insist on a down payment of fifty per cent with order, the balance being paid on delivery.

If you happened to be a multi-millionaire, your standard of living probably wouldn't alter very much. Unfortunately, most of us are not millionaires; therefore we would suffer by varying degrees relevant to our own social grouping. The reason social grouping is important is that the abolition of credit would have a disproportionate effect on the working and lower-middle classes, for the following reasons:

☐ Most of the mass-produced goods in this country are luxury items. Without mass production the manufacturing cost for each item produced would increase dramatically. This would result in the goods being priced outside the budget of working and lower middle class families.

☐ It is usually people from these social groups who purchase luxury items on credit. Without the availability of credit, even if prices remained stable they could not afford to purchase these items.

☐ Despite the computer revolution, mass production still creates a large number of low-paid, semi-skilled jobs. These jobs are usually filled by the working and lower-middle class populace. Without the mass-production of luxury items these jobs would disappear. This would cause a rapid increase in the level of unemployment for these social groups.

As well as the luxury items listed above, you would also lose the ability to purchase items of necessity. How many of you could afford to purchase your home without the aid of a mortgage? If you are thinking of overcoming this problem by renting a council property, you should think again. At present, councils are reducing their housing stock, despite an ever-increasing waiting list, and your chances of securing one would be very slim.

The only other option is to rent through the private sector. However, the sudden increase in demand for these properties would undoubtedly lead to a rapid increase in monthly rents. It could cost you more each month to rent than your original mortgage.

Even in this greatly oversimplified view– and we have hardly yet scratched the surface – it is easy to see how important credit is to each and every one of us. Without it, society would quickly revert to the old class system, with all the poverty, ill-health and poor education that went with it.

The role of the Credit Control department

Life 'as we know it' could not exist without some form of credit. But if you are going to offer credit, you need to develop some way of controlling it; this is where you and I enter the picture. The responsibility for controlling credit and turning promises into hard cash falls to people like us: Credit Controllers. So how can we start to control it?

As things stand, it is difficult to give a definitive answer to this question: 'credit control' can mean different things to different companies and different industries. The one thing they all have in common is the need to collect money quickly for the goods they have sold on credit. For my own part, I believe the role of the credit control department is to maximise sales while minimizing the risk of bad debts. The remainder of this book is dedicated to the way this can be achieved.

Over the years I have found that credit control is often an enigma to senior management and sales staff alike. Although times are changing, some companies still see the credit control function as a dangerous area, shrouded in a cloak of mystery. This usually occurs in companies where the credit function is not very well defined, and the credit manager feels he has to complicate the functions of his department to justify his existence.

In other companies, you may well find that the credit control and sales departments are virtually at war with one another. This attitude is of no benefit to anyone, and needs to be overcome before progress can be made in developing credit control as a genuine profit centre – just like sales, in fact. This type of friction usually stems from ignorance of interdepartmental needs, and a refusal to appreciate the role each function has to play in a successful trading company.

One of the most common misapprehensions sales people seem to have about credit control is that it loses their company valued customers. In my experience, the chances of this happening are few and far between. I believe wholeheartedly that – when carried out in a professional manner – credit control can actually increase a company's sales. Collecting debts while maintaining customer goodwill is imperative if a company is to grow and prosper. This belief will be carved deep into the heart of every successful credit controller.

The role of the credit controller is a high-pressure one, and at times can be very lonely. If you are going to succeed in this profession, you need to be able to stand your ground and be prepared to explain the reasoning behind your decisions, even at the highest level. You will find that the more successful you are, the more you will be noticed; and the more you are noticed, the more your actions and decisions will be questioned. Being able to do the job well is only part of the credit controller's brief. He also needs to be able to explain clearly and concisely why he is doing a good job. As for the credit manager, his is the perpetual high-wire act, trying to balance the need for sales against the need to collect overdue accounts. The strain in trying to achieve this balance, especially in times of recession, can become unbearable. A company cannot survive without being able to sell its goods or services. At the same time it cannot survive without collecting the money owed to it.

Offering credit is a risky business. A company that sells goods on credit is gambling that its credit controllers will be able to collect its debts before they become so old that there is no profit left in the sale. No company offers credit to its customers expecting all of them to pay on 30 days, and no credit control department should set out with this as its goal. Aiming this high can only lead to poor performance, as your collection techniques would have to be so aggressive that they would undoubtedly be harmful to the company's sales function. The company has taken the decision to accept the risk of selling on credit: your job is not to eliminate that risk – it is to manage it.

The role of the credit manager is undoubtedly taking on a new level of importance, for reasons which I shall go into later. Nowadays, he (being male, I have used the masculine pronoun throughout this book to avoid the clumsy 'he or she', but you know who I mean) needs to be a good communicator with people at all levels, from the tea lady right up to the managing director. His first task, then, is to use this skill to spread the gospel, and to try to convert as many people in the organisation as possible to the religion of effective credit control. This conversion process should start at the top and work its way downwards and outwards; the financial director will – or should – already be aware of the benefits an effectively run credit control function can bring.

Therefore, the conversion process should more effectively start with the sales director and work down through the sales managers, financial controllers, group accountants and sales staff.

Most of your inter-company contact will in fact take place with sales staff; therefore it is imperative that you try to educate them in the benefits they will receive from an effective credit control system. If you fail, they will continue to have a stereotyped vision of how a credit controller operates and it will be very difficult to build up any kind of effective working relationship. Left to their own imagination, they suspect that we normally pick up the phone with sparks flying, threatening all kinds of dire consequences and browbeating their customers into submission. As we all know, nothing could be further from the truth; there are very few people in this world whom you can actually frighten into paying your account. (Unless, of course, you are intending to 'send the boys round', a procedure which I must advise you straight away is highly illegal and not recommended...)

A sales person and a credit controller are in fact closely related animals of the same species. The first phone call made by both sales staff and credit controllers is effectively the same call: it will usually be a cold call, made to a stranger with the express intention of selling something – the one trying to sell a product or a service, the other trying to sell the idea of paying an overdue account: both are after the customer's money, which he is reluctant to part with. At the end of the day, the credit controller has a bigger stick with which to persuade the customer who is unresponsive; but this action would not be taken until the later stages of the chase cycle.

Credit management, if it is allowed to operate to its full potential, is a logical process designed to collect the maximum amount of money possible over a given time-frame. The first phase of the credit cycle starts with the application of credit itself. The second phase takes the form of a two-way communication with the debtor by phone and letter. The third and final phase is where you have to put on your debt collector's hat, and get tough with the debtor; however, if you are carrying out your job correctly, only a small percentage of debtors will reach the third stage. (A full description of the three phases of credit control can be found in Chapter 4.)

There is no doubt that the role and importance of the credit manager have benefited from the recessions of the 'eighties and early 'nineties. The desperate need of companies to collect money urgently, and the worrying level of bankruptcies and liquidations, helped to focus the spotlight on the need for, and obvious benefit to be gained from, effective credit control. This was especially true of the small business sector which, during both recessions, found it almost impossible to obtain from the banks, the level of financing necessary to keep their businesses afloat. This made it imperative that cash was generated from credit sales as quickly as possible, in order to help finance the day-to-day running of the business.

Now that the economy has moved out of recession, some companies probably feel they can now relax their credit control policies. However, if they want to take advantage of the boom part of the trading cycle, nothing could be further from the truth. It is not only in times of recession that credit control is important. Even in boom years, business growth still needs to be financed. A high level of growth mixed with poor credit control makes a deadly cocktail that can lead to severe long-term cash flow problems, high borrowing costs in the form of bank overdrafts or short term loans and, ultimately, to the demise of the company.

The changing face of credit control

The role and functions of the credit control department are changing. In recent years it has developed its own identity, to match its new levels of responsibility. Hopefully within the next decade, credit control departments across the country will have broken free from the shackles of their 'accounts department' association and will be standing alone as a totally independent function reporting directly at board level.

This new-found identity will allow the credit control department a more direct input into the formation of the company's credit policy. This is essential if we are to counter the commercial changes that have taken place over the last few years. In today's high-tech, full-throttle world of commerce, debt avoidance is a much more sophisticated game. This has led to the need for a new class of employee: a better educated, more sophisticated credit controller, capable of collecting the high level of debts needed to oil the wheels of the business world, enabling it to churn on in a self-perpetuating cycle of sales and profits.

Any successful credit control department of the future must be highly motivated in its attitude and highly professional in its outlook; these attributes are essential if it is to bridge the divide between the requirements and expectations of credit control, past and future. This new professionalism and motivation will be achieved only if the function has its own identity with which the credit controller can associate. There are no hard-and-fast rules as far as credit control is concerned; its decision-making needs to be fluid and 'of the moment'. It cannot operate effectively within the delays and rigidity of the accounts department, where it will always come a poor second to the management accounts function in the allocation of time and resources .

As the role of the credit controller changes, so the skills of the individual credit controller need to evolve. In the past, people would drift into credit control with no prior knowledge or experience in the field. Some would find their professional niche in life, develop their skills and progress. Unfortunately, the majority would tread water for a couple of years, with no real understanding or interest in their role, and then move on to new roles within the accounts function.

As is often the case, it was this ill-fated majority that cast the die for the role of the credit controller. This stereotype of a credit controller has probably done more to harm the professional standing of the industry than any other single factor. Without doubt, I believe it is the main reason why the credit control function has still to fulfil its true potential within the organisational hierarchy.

It was the recession of the early 'nineties that finally changed the role of the credit controller forever. Directors and proprietors of both large and small businesses became acutely aware of the importance of collecting money quickly and efficiently, without losing customer goodwill. More importantly, they were prepared to pay a high level of salary for credit managers and controllers who could achieve this. As a result, at a time when most management professionals were finding their salaries frozen or even reduced, good credit managers and controllers were moving up the pay league.

The higher salaries that became available had a twofold effect on the recruitment of credit personnel: first, they attracted a better quality of candidate. Secondly, credit managers, eager to preserve their new-found level of professionalism, became a lot more choosy about the staff they employed.

If credit management is to take its rightful place within the managerial hierarchy it needs to continue this encouraging development well into the next decade. The only way this can be achieved is by developing the ability of young credit controllers. They will be the credit managers of the future, and in their hands lies the destiny of our profession. Never again should we allow the 'flotsam and jetsam' to infiltrate our profession; for we are now truly a profession, with substantial rewards for those who are willing to work hard and succeed.

As a profession, we should be pressing employers to offer their credit controllers study packages similar to those on offer to management accountants and other disciplines. This would enable credit managers to insist that all junior controllers enrol as students of the Institute of Credit Management, and sit their professional exams. Industry could then grade credit controllers as Junior, Part-Qualified, and Qualified, allowing companies to set a more uniform wage structure.

Above all, perhaps, we could give our profession a clearly defined career path; which is the one thing that still sets us apart from other bodies such as the accounting and legal professions. Once this has been achieved, we will be able to encourage school and college leavers to make a positive step towards a career in credit control; and as a profession, we will at last have come of age.

2

THE PSYCHOLOGY OF CREDIT CONTROL

The credit control function operates at varying levels across the world of commerce. The level at which it operates within your company will depend on the credit policies laid down by the executive directors and the vision and communication skills of your credit manager.

At its lowest level, credit control is nothing more than the occasional chasing of debts mixed in with other sales ledger duties. At its highest, though, it is a war of attrition; incorporating all the planning and strategy normally associated with a successful military campaign. It is here, at the highest elevation of the credit controller's art, that you will come across an understanding and deliberate use of the psychology of debt collection – The Holy Grail, sought by only the purest of credit managers, to help achieve the best collection results possible.

Slowly, over the centuries, society's treatment of the debtor has become more lenient. In Biblical times, the non-payment of a debt was considered theft and was punishable by having your hands chopped off. Every seven years, an amnesty would be declared in order to ensure that sufficient able-bodied men were left who could carry a sword! In this country, in the early nineteenth century, a debtor could be thrown into debtor's prison and left there to rot until such time as his or her debts were cleared. As recently as the early 'seventies, people could still be shamed into paying their accounts;

holding on to other people's money was generally considered anti-social. Now all that has changed, thanks to the ubiquitous credit card. In today's credit-ridden trading conditions, debt avoidance has become a much more sophisticated game – a game where the use of psychology is needed to fill the chasm left by society's declining standards of financial morality.

Given that debtors can no longer be shamed into paying their accounts, the effective credit controller has to find other keys that can be used to unlock the door to payment. Every debtor needs to be treated as an individual; therefore, it follows that you need to find their own individual key. For example, you may be able to frighten the proprietor of a small business into paying your account with the threat of legal action, but this strategy will not work on a large multinational corporation.

The psychology of the chase call

Each debtor's own particular payment 'key' will be found only by probing their psyche in a systematic and controlled manner. As you read through this chapter, you will start to realise that you already apply psychology within your normal chase cycle. However, this second-hand usage is not enough. To obtain the maximum effect, psychology needs to be applied in a deliberate and controlled manner.

The first psychological probe you will use will be your chase cycle or, to be more precise, the content of and delay between each element of the cycle. Studies into the effects of telephone chase cycles have shown that the optimum time lag between each level of contact is seven days. This allows the debtor time to absorb and think about the content of the call. The initial reaction of your debtor during your 'phone conversation may be one of total indifference, and you may well end the call feeling that you have not secured payment. However, seven days allows plenty of time for the debtor to change his mind, and quite often he does.

This situation usually manifests itself when the debtor finds it impossible to admit that he is in the wrong. He finds it very difficult to back down on the phone and admit that you have every right to expect him to pay the debt. However, given the opportunity to calm down for a few days and think things over without anyone confronting him, he can convince his ego that he is making the decision to pay your account of his own free will.

Some credit controllers seem to think the best way to obtain payment is to call their debtors every two days and try to wear down their resistance; this is not a very professional approach to the collection of overdue debts. In most cases it will also be unproductive, as your debtor will not have had time to come to terms with paying your account and, by calling frequently, you are merely increasing his resistance. In this situation the debtor must be allowed a little time to convince himself that he should pay your debt, otherwise he will simply dig his heels in even further.

Not only is this type of constant chasing laying you open to a charge of harassment, it also denies the debtor time to consider the benefits of paying your account. Constant harassment will eventually lead to a confrontation in which your debtor either has to give in to your demands and lose face, or take a stand and delay payment of your account even further. It is not part of our human make-up to accept loss of face easily; therefore, nine times out of ten, your debtor will decide to save face and take the second option. Once this happens, the non-payment of your debt becomes a matter of principle to your debtor, and this really is the last thing you want to happen.

If you allow debt avoidance to become a matter of principle, your debtor will be able to convince himself that he is doing all the wrong things for all the right reasons. Having allowed the situation to reach this stage there is no way back; you will be left with no option other than to proceed with legal action. This action will be costly and time-consuming for everyone, and probably could have been avoided if you had approached the chasing of the debt in a less confrontational manner.

One of the secrets of effective cash collection is to apply enough pressure on the debtor to make life uncomfortable, without pushing him over the edge. If you back any animal into a corner with no way of escape, their natural instinct will be to attack... Easy does it.

When chasing your debtor for payment you should try to isolate him from any reasonable excuse for not paying the debt. By stripping away the excuses one by one, he eventually has nowhere to hide and has to admit liability for the debt. I am not saying that you will always be able to avoid a confrontation – sometimes there is no other option. However, you should remember that your sales department will want to deal with this customer again. With this in mind, a more persuasive approach must be the best long-term option for your company's survival.

You should not allow your personal feelings towards your debtor to influence the way you approach the collection of your debt. It is almost second nature to fall into a negative thought pattern when you have continually to chase a difficult debtor for payment. It is very easy to feel sympathy towards a debtor who is nice and polite each time you call, and quite openly admits that he has a temporary cash flow problem. No-one, however, has sympathy for the debtor who is argumentative on the phone and elusive about when he will be able to send you a cheque.

Both of the above debtors are suffering from the effects of poor cash flow. Neither of them has given you a firm date for payment, so why are you more positive about phoning Mrs Nice, than you are about calling Mr Nasty? The only thing that separates these debtors is the mental barrier that you are rapidly erecting against Mr Nasty. I know it is more difficult to speak to this character, but you should remember that he is probably under severe stress, and anything he says is not personally aimed at you. In these circumstances you need to remove yourself from the picture and view the situation as a spectator; this allows you to make decisions in a calmer, more rational state of mind.

When you speak to a debtor who is experiencing problems, you should try to convince him that you understand his problems and want to help wherever possible. Imagine you are walking home one night and come across a man preparing to commit suicide by jumping from a bridge; you may feel that he is a loser, and that he does not have a hope of making anything of his life, but would you choose this moment to go over and tell him this to his face? Well, you might if you were Dirty Harry, but he is the exception that proves the rule.

Faced with this situation, you would probably listen to what the man has to say, and sympathise with his problems. Then you would try to emphasise all the good things in his life, in the belief that you could make him feel that there was hope. Above all, you would try to make him feel that he is valued.

The way you react to someone who is about to jump is exactly the way you should react to a debtor who has cash flow problems; he may not be jumping off a bridge, but he could be drowning just the same.

When speaking to a slow-paying customer you should never dismiss his problems as being irrelevant. They may be to you, but they certainly are not to him. This type of reply will push the debtor into a defensive frame of mind, and will undoubtedly result in a negative response. You should sympathise with his problems and try to offer ways to resolve them that will be of benefit to you both. Explain to him how important he is to your company, and how each party benefits from the trading relationship.

What you should not do is dump all your problems on to him. By this I mean that you should not use phrases such as:

☐ "we are all under pressure. We need to collect our money just as urgently as you do"
☐ "I have targets to reach as well, and that means I need to collect this debt."
☐ "If I don't collect the money owed to us my job is on the line."

Your debtor has no interest in your problems, and if you respond in this way he will jump.

Escalating the situation

When making your chase call you should always be prepared to escalate the situation if necessary. It is pointless calling the bought ledger clerk week after week, chasing the elusive payment that never comes. First and foremost, he will not be the decision-maker – and as such will not be able to authorise payment of your account. Secondly, he spends his whole life fending off credit controllers who are chasing for payment, therefore it is safe to assume he is fairly at ease with this.

Having reached this stage of your chase cycle you should escalate the situation and move your chase activity up a level or two. If you now speak to the group accountant or the financial controller you may find things are a little different.

People who operate at this level do not spend much, if any, of their time dealing with credit controllers chasing overdue accounts, therefore it is unlikely that they will be well schooled in the art of fending off requests for payment. By placing these people in a position where they have to deal with this problem, you are forcing them to operate outside their comfort zone. Like everyone else, they are more susceptible to outside influences when not totally in control of the situation.

More often than not, a second phone call to this person will result in your debt being paid. They will pay you simply because they feel uncomfortable at having to deal with you. This feeling of insecurity will increase if they have tried to avoid your calls, but you have still managed to get through to them.

Having escalated the situation, you should not go back to speaking to the bought ledger clerk; keep trying to contact the financial controller. Even if you are not getting through, your messages will be. The fact that you refuse to go away will be increasing the pressure on him and, if all else fails, you should send your letter threatening legal action marked for his personal attention.

The worst problem I have when trying to collect debts owed to my company is obtaining payment from small limited companies. These companies are often capitalised with two £1 shares and obtain the necessary working capital to survive only by delaying payment to their creditors. Unfortunately, they are also the worst at controlling their own debtors, creating a vicious circle. It is this type of debtor who usually has no assets on which to levy, when you try to enforce judgement. However, this does not have to be the end of the matter.

You can increase the psychological pressure being placed on your debtor by contacting him at home regarding his overdue debt. This works very well on directors of limited companies who think they can hide behind their limited liability. We all consider our home to be our castle, the last bastion from the reality of the outside world. If you breach this bastion you really do disarm the debtor. All he wants to do then is repel you from his private space. He does not want the reality of his business world invading his private life; he does not want to accept that there really is no hiding place from his responsibilities – he is even prepared to pay you to get you off his back.

I have personally experienced cases where this has happened, and for the price of a phone call or a letter it has got to be worth a try.

The psychology of the collection letter

Which is the most important element of the chase letter? Those of you who said the content, go to the bottom of the class! When a debtor opens a chase letter and looks at it, it is not the content that grabs his attention, at this stage he has not had a chance to read the letter. The thing that attracts the debtor's attention and makes him decide whether he is going to read it, or just throw it in the bin, is the letter's visual impact.

If the letter looks important or official and is personal to him, he will read it. If it looks like another computer-generated chase letter, he will simply throw it away. It does not matter whether the letter is the first or the last in your chase cycle, always make it look important. It should also look as if it has been written personally for that debtor. Once you have convinced the debtor to read your letter, then obviously the content of the letter becomes important.

The visual impact of the letters you send to your customer plays a most important part in the psychological pressure you are trying to inflict on him. How often have you placed an account into the hands of a collection agency, only to find that a reasonable percentage of these debts are paid within a few days? Of course, the account was chased thoroughly by you for several weeks with no positive result before being handed out. Now, however, the debtor sees the initial letter from the collection agency, with their name blazoned across the top; he has got to know you well, but these are strangers to him; he does not know how powerful they might be. He starts to visualise nasty things happening to him if he does not clear your account: he resigns the game and pays.

This psychological response is a useful tool for focusing your debtor's mind on the problem at hand; and, in fact, it can be provoked without having to send your accounts to a collection agency at all. As the final stage of your chase cycle, you should send out a letter to your debtor headed in bold type, 'Debt Recovery Enforcement Department'. This letter should also be signed: 'Legal Controller', to emphasise its importance; and printed on good quality grey paper, as this drab colour creates a feeling of hopelessness and demoralisation in the debtor's mind.

This letter works on your debtor's psyche in exactly the same way as the collection agency's letter, making him feel that things are becoming serious and must be resolved. In tests carried out by my credit control department, this letter achieved a 30 per cent success rate when used as the last step of the collection cycle.

The psychology of staff motivation

The implementation of psychology in the credit control department has a number of uses, and does not need to be restricted to a purely negative role. The innovative credit manager will also use psychology to hone his team into a coherent fighting force.

One of the most important factors relating to a credit controller's well-being is the environment in which he works. His level of output will definitely be enhanced if the office is well lit by natural light, and adequate space is allocated to each credit controller. The state and colour of the office decor are also important. Credit control is a pressured and stressful occupation, but an office that is decorated in relaxing colours will help to reduce the level of stress and result in increased output.

The style of management deployed in the running of the department is also of great importance. In the past I have experienced managerial styles whereby staff were chastised if they performed badly, and ignored when they performed well. This form of management is archaic and unproductive. You cannot frighten people into performing well. If performance is not what it should be, then you need to discuss the problem with your team and decide on a course of action to improve matters. The team should be involved in the development of collection policy because it has been proved, time and again, that people work harder to achieve a goal which they themselves have been involved in setting than they do when the goal has merely been imposed upon them. (Further reference to this subject can be found in Chapter 10.)

Another facet of the human psyche that can be used to increase performance is our fundamental need to belong to the community. We all have an inherent longing to be part of a team, and the cost of entry has to be a solid working performance. If a good team spirit can be developed in the office and socially outside work, this will help to raise output and enhance success.

The more experience you gain in this profession, the greater will be your understanding of what makes a debtor tick. By implementing psychology into the debt collection process at the right juncture, your collection performance can only improve.

3

THE ESSENCE OF CREDIT CONTROL

One of the most powerful forces in the universe exists within each and every one of us: the 'power of thought'....

As Henry Ford said: "Whether you think you will, or whether you think you won't, you'll be right." What he meant was that we are each a product of our expectations. If we approach something in a negative way, we have to expect a negative response. This is certainly true when dealing with the collection of overdue debts; if you approach a collection call not expecting to collect the debt, it can hardly come as a surprise to you when you are not successful. If you do not believe in yourself and what you are saying, why should anyone else? If you want to be successful in this profession, it is imperative that you believe in your own ability.

So how do you develop the necessary confidence to be truly successful when collecting debts? If you take a more detailed look at confidence itself, you will find it is made up of three elements: knowledge, motivation, and a supportive system. These elements interact with each other to form a solid foundation upon which every successful credit control department is built. Let us now take a look at each of these individual elements in turn.

Knowledge

There are many areas of knowledge that credit controllers take for granted in their normal working day. Every credit controller expects to know who has paid their account and who has not; how overdue a given debt is; and the address and phone number of their customers, so that they can be contacted. This type of knowledge is essential, and it goes without saying that every credit control department in the country should have this information readily available. The knowledge I want to talk about in this section could be classed as 'third dimensional' – knowledge that will add detail to the routine information and form part of the foundation that will help to create the level of confidence required to make a successful call.

The first piece of knowledge you need to acquire as a credit controller is your company's corporate policy regarding the collection of overdue debts. You need to know what time-frame your company expects you to work within, and what lengths it is prepared to go to, to collect its money. There is no point in threatening your debtors with some form of action that you know your company is not prepared to carry out.

The debtor must believe that if you say you are going to do something you will follow it through, and that your company is prepared to back your decisions. For this reason, it is important that you do not overstep your level of authority; as this can only result in you losing all credibility with your customers. If a credit control department does not have credibility, then it has nothing; it cannot perform successfully.

You also need a working knowledge of the law relating to credit control and insolvency. You do not need to be able to quote chapter and verse from the Insolvency Act 1986, but you do need to know when the debtor is trying to con you. If you do not have this knowledge you will find the debtor will say something that you find it impossible to respond to.

Another crucial area of knowledge is how important your goods or services are to your customer. The greater his need for your goods, the more influence you have over him. (This thought is developed further in Chapter 6.)

Knowing why your debtor is paying you late is also very important. Until you know the reason for the slow payment, you cannot deal with it; each reason for slow payment needs to be dealt with in a slightly different way.

One of the main reasons for slow payment is under-capitalisation. This is a problem that is usually restricted to small businesses which find it difficult, or are unwilling, to inject adequate sums of capital into their business to finance their trading activities.

This problem has its roots firmly planted in the early 1980s when the economy shifted into recession and unemployment grew to over three million. The newly-elected Thatcher government was keen to do everything in its power to encourage the growing army of state dependents to set up businesses of their own. Their aim was to reduce the level of unemployment, and at the same time reduce the social security budget. This policy was inspirational until the government's fiscal policy of the late 'eighties caused the economy to overheat and, as a result, heralded a second recession; the worst this country has known since the depression of the 'thirties.

Just prior to the start of the last recession, 97 per cent of all businesses in the country employed twenty staff or less, and this is probably one reason why the recession bit so deeply. Suddenly, for the first time since their inception, these White Knights of the Thatcherite dream were floundering. The recession had shown up the inadequacies of these businesses, so many of which were capitalized by just two £1 shares. With no other long-term investment by the directors, this in turn led to difficulties in obtaining finance through bank loans or overdrafts. As a result they were able to survive only by running their business on their creditors' money.

Companies that are under-capitalized tend to use open-ended excuses to delay payment. An open-ended excuse is one that is not restricted by any time limit; for example, a copy invoice request can turn into a request for proof of delivery, or a dispute over the authorisation of the purchase.

Some other examples of open-ended excuses are: "The cheque is in the post", "There's no-one available at present to sign the cheque", "The director has broken his arm and cannot sign the cheque", "The office has been damaged by fire, we are waiting for the insurance money to come through" and: "The office was broken into last night and all the invoices were stolen". (I can scarcely imagine why anyone would want to break into an office and steal invoices, but you would be surprised how often it happens!) All of these excuses can sound plausible and, as they appear to suggest that payment will be received shortly, they are easy to accept. This type of debtor is usually distinguishable by their payment pattern, which may start off on time, but gets progressively slower, month after month.

When making phone calls to this type of debtor, you should use the knowledge you have gained of the company, and begin your phone call by asking:

> "Mr Smith, I notice from our records that your payments are being made later and later each month. Could you tell me if there is any reason for this?"

Hopefully this will enable you to by-pass all the open-ended excuses and cut to the real problem, which will probably be insufficient cash flow. Arriving at the real problem early on in the chase cycle will not make the debtor any more able to pay your account; the sooner you tackle the real problem and start to resolve it, however, the sooner the debt will be cleared.

The second reason people tend to pay you late is because they are cash-managing your money. Many years ago it was considered a smear on one's character if you did not honour your debts; in fact, unless you had good reason for withholding payment, you could end up being imprisoned until such time as they were cleared. Now, no matter how much we like the idea of our elusive debtors being incarcerated, we can't do that; and no bad thing. Debtors' prison was not only harsh justice, it was also counter-productive, as it is almost impossible to raise money to clear one's debts while rotting behind bars. I do feel, though, that it is still morally wrong when a society does not consider it important to honour its debts. If all debts were paid on time, the free flow of funds from business to business would generate an enormous boost to the economy.

Companies that are cash-managing your money can actually afford to pay your account on time. The reason they keep your money in their bank account is simply to reduce their overdraft charges and increase their profits. These companies usually have highly trained payable managers or clerks whose job it is to keep you at bay for as long as possible; thereby enabling your debtors to pay on their credit terms and not yours.

You can spot companies that are cash-managing your money because they all tend to pay their accounts at the same time each month. Where under-capitalized companies use open-ended excuses to delay payment, companies that are cash-managing your money will use closed-ended excuses. This means they use excuses that have a definite end date, such as: "We only raise cheques on the eighteenth of the month", "You are on the next cheque run", "We only have one cheque run a month", "We operate 60/90/120 day terms with all our suppliers..." Once again, these excuses are easy to accept because they imply a firm payment date and will often be successful when used against the unprepared credit controller.

Using the knowledge you have obtained on this debtor you should start your call by asking:

> "Mr Smith from our records I notice you are paying your account on 65 days when our terms clearly state that payment is due on 30 days. Is there any reason why you can't pay us on 30 days?"

By tying the debtor down to a specific question in this way you should uncover the real reason for delayed payment with your first call, which is very important if you wish to reduce your days' sales outstanding (DSO) figure.

This type of question will usually be met with a response from the debtor that will go something like:

> *"It is our company policy to pay accounts on 65-day terms. You can't expect us to pay our accounts on time when people don't pay us until 60 days."*

At this stage you should not fall into the trap of telling the debtor how he should be running his business, if you do you will be entering into an argument that you cannot possibly win. You should agree that how and when he pays his other creditors is entirely up to him, but where your account is concerned you expect him to adhere to your agreed credit terms. You should then go on to sell him the special benefits he receives through being able to trade with your company.

There is no point in making this type of call to a bought ledger clerk, as only a decision-maker can alter the company's payment terms. It should also be remembered that the more important your goods or services are to your debtor, the more successful you will be in reducing his payment days.

The third type of delayed payment will arise from a debtor who has a grievance. A grievance is a complaint – it is not an excuse to delay payment. It is very important that you learn to differentiate between the two. For example, a spelling mistake in an advertisement that does not detract from its commercial value may be annoying, but it is not a reason for refusing to pay the invoice. If on the other hand you had contracted to run your client's advertisement on the inside cover of your publication, which is a prime position, and in fact had placed it on page ten, then your customer has a genuine reason to withhold payment. In this case the commercial value of his advertisement has obviously been impaired and some form of compensation is due.

When you are faced with a customer who has a grievance, you need to be very careful how you proceed with the call. If you try to marginalise his grievance, you will be adding fuel to the fire. You will find then that all the anger your customer feels will be laid at your door.

When dealing with this type of customer, you should trade the extended credit your debtor has taken against the 'value' of his grievance. Even before you make this call you know your customer is going to give you a hard time. He wants to get even for all the aggravation you have caused him. So, before you call them, remind yourself that this is a good customer who has a genuine grievance; he is not a debtor who is merely trying to find an excuse to delay payment. If you approach this call in the wrong way, you could lose the customer forever.

A grievance call should go something like:

"Hello, Mr Smith, this is Michael Cannon from XYZ Ltd. I am calling you regarding payment of your May invoice. I understand from our sales department that there was a mix-up with your order, and I presume this is the reason you haven't paid your account yet?"

"That's right, and I don't see why I should go out of my way to pay your account. Your error wasted a lot of my time."

"I fully appreciate how you feel Mr Smith, and that is why I have not chased for payment of this invoice. I have spoken to our sales department, and they assure me that there will not be a reoccurrence of this problem. Mr Smith, we would hate to think that this error could damage our trading relationship."

"Okay, I'll put a cheque in the post for you tonight, but remember I do not expect a reoccurrence of this problem."

Mr Smith was obviously not happy, but when approached in this way, provided he needs your goods or services, he will pay. If Mr Smith only purchases goods from you once a year, you will probably have a lot more trouble obtaining payment.

By linking the error on Mr Smith's order with the delay in his payment, you were trading one off against the other, by reminding him that the error has also cost you money. The fact that Mr Smith may always take extended credit when he pays his account is of no relevance. He believes he has exchanged extended credit in return for your error. He is now even and that is all that matters to him.

A supportive system

The second factor needed to create confidence is a supportive system.

A supportive system can be broken down into two elements: first, there is the actual hardware you use in your day-to-day chase activity. Secondly, there is the support you receive from other colleagues in the accounts and sales departments. Both of these elements are important if you are to create the confidence necessary to be successful.

Hardware Support

Every company should supply its credit control department with an aged debtors list, a chase history and a 'phone. These are the bare essentials necessary to allow the department to function.

In my first credit control job, that was just about all the company did supply, with the exception of the mandatory desk and chair (fixed back, with no height adjustment – not up to today's EU regulations).

Today, you will find that the credit control department is usually a little better equipped. Many will now operate collection software, customised to meet their very own needs. The company I work for has recently developed its own credit control module, offering options that are light years away from anything that was on offer when I started in this business. Our collection module has a diarised chase system which lists all the calls that need to be made that day. The calls are also broken down into their contact levels, i.e., first call, second call, first letter, etc. This prevents any debtor slipping down the join in the paper, which always seemed to happen with the old-fashioned debtors' list.

Once a call is made, the account is automatically tagged with the next contact date and level. Every account has an on-line chase history that has to be updated at the end of each call. At the touch of a button you can view the debtor's payment history, obtain an aged breakdown of the account, or print a hard copy. Copy invoices are produced without having to leave your chair (the laser printer producing a better quality copy than the original.) Chase letters are printed automatically each day. A 'search' facility allows you to search by account number, name, phone number, invoice number, or cheque number. At present we are developing the facility to enable us to fax copy invoices direct from the screen, and create computerised journals and collection agency forms.

This system has helped considerably to reduce our admin and call preparation time, allowing us to invest more of our time in making those all-important chase calls. As there is a proven link between the number of chase calls made and the amount of cash received, using our new system has helped us to achieve a substantial reduction in our overdue debtors figure.

Support From Other Departments

Unfortunately, a state-of-the-art collection system is not enough, as credit control is not a stand-alone function. It needs the support of the sales ledger and sales departments if it is to operate at its optimum level.

Until an invoice appears as overdue on a debtors' listing, a credit controller will not have had any opportunity to influence what has happened to it. Therefore you need to have complete faith that the sales person and sales ledger department have carried out their tasks correctly. We are human, we all make mistakes – the odd error should not detract from a credit controller's confidence in making an effective collection call. The problem arises when the same mistakes and failures are occurring, time after time, without any action being taken to put them right. This is when credit controllers will begin to have doubts about the validity of the debts they are chasing, and subconsciously their calls will become less assertive.

If a credit controller is going to be effective, he must believe fully in the debt he is chasing. Continually having to apologise to debtors for mistakes that have been made is demotivating, and will prevent you from remaining in control of the conversation, which is a prerequisite for a successful collection call.

It is not only errors in the selling or invoicing processes that cause problems for credit controllers. A fault in the accounting system that is not rectified can also create horrifying collection problems, as I know from personal experience.

One of the companies I worked for in my dim and distant past had a system of filing their sales invoices in date order, as opposed to numerically. This meant that if you wanted to supply a customer with a copy invoice, you needed to know which day the relevant sale was made. To add to the confusion, nobody could agree whether invoices should be batched and filed by the date they were raised or by the date on which they were posted to the system.

The result of this confusion was that we had to employ two credit control clerks, who spent their whole day trying to locate copy invoices. As things got progressively worse, it was taking us anything up to one month to supply a copy invoice. As word spread among our customers, everybody seemed to be asking for copies... Every time a credit controller made a collection call he expected to be asked for a copy invoice, and knew straight away that the debtor had just bought himself another four weeks extended credit.

How assertive do you think those credit controllers were when making their chase calls?

Motivation

The last factor needed to create confidence is motivation. Any credit control department that is going to produce high quality results, month after month, has to be highly motivated. It is very important for all credit managers to realise that credit controllers do not perform well simply because they are paid a wage. They come to work because they are paid a wage, but they perform well because they are *motivated*.

Many managers apparently believe that it is their job to change their employees, and to instil this thing called 'motivation', which will enable them to behave the way the company perceives they should. Unfortunately, they seldom do; you cannot 'give' someone motivation, it already exists within each and every one of us. The job of a credit manager is to devise ways to stimulate and bring out this inherent motivation in his credit controllers; not to try and impose it.

More than fifty years ago, psychologist Abraham Maslow identi-fied the five basic categories of personal motivation. He also proposed that, as individuals, we all react differently to each of these motives.

Therefore, motivation can only be achieved by matching the correct motive to the correct individual and stimulating them accordingly. The five motives he categorized are as follows.

☐ Survival
☐ Safety & security
☐ Need to belong
☐ Self-esteem
☐ Self-development.

I think we can assume that all credit controllers achieve the basic survival needs, i.e., food, water, air, and shelter. Therefore I will ignore this category and concentrate on the remaining four motives:

Safety & security

During the last recession, companies were falling like ninepins. There were over three million people unemployed, and very few new jobs were being created. During this period, individual safety and security were of prime importance. Companies that could offer a measure of security were well on the way to having a highly motivated work force. However, in times of normal trading, when people are happy to move from company to company, safety & security will not be very high on the list of performance enhancing motives.

Need to belong

We all need social interaction, needing to belong. Managers faced with employees that fit into this category need to develop good interpersonal relationships with them. Another way to motivate this type of employee is to create a team activity that they can contribute to. This type of employee will always give more to team activities than to individual tasks.

Self-esteem

Many employees are driven by the need to prove they are worthwhile and that, as individuals, they have an important part to play. The easiest way to motivate this type of employee is to catch them doing something right, and praise them for it. Setting up systems to enable this type of credit controller to measure his own performance is an ideal way of increasing his performance level.

Self-development

Maslow thought that this was the highest level of human motivation – the desire to reach the unreachable star, to develop one's ability to the full. Managers can stimulate this motive by sending employees on internal and external training courses. It would also be beneficial to give them projects to work on that will enable them to develop new skills.

You cannot expect to become supremely confident and highly effective overnight. There is an art to collecting debts that will only come with experience. Above all, you will develop a sixth sense when it comes to judging a debtor's response to your request for payment. Learn to have faith in your convictions. Your first impression is usually the correct one.

Enjoyment in your work will come from success, from setting goals and achieving them. Credit control is a profession, requiring a scientific response to a particular problem that needs thought, dedication, and courage if it is to be carried out correctly

Credit control is not for the faint-hearted. You have to become accustomed to being out on a limb. There are many times that I have stared into the eyes of midnight, desperately trying to find a way to resolve a particular problem. It is at times like this that you have to fall back on your belief in your own ability and cling to your convictions.

Credit control is the most rewarding, yet the most demoralising; the simplest, yet the most complicated profession I have ever come across. However, if you believe in yourself and the importance of what you are trying to achieve, you are taking the first steps along the road to achievement, fulfilment and unassailable success.

4

CHASING OVERDUE ACCOUNTS

For many years the only medium used for the chasing of outstanding debts was the Overdue Letter. When it was socially unacceptable to default on your debts, that was all that was needed to generate payment. However, in today's high-tech, full-throttle world of commerce, debt avoidance is a much more sophisticated game. Although I still feel there is a place for the debt collection letter within a modern day chase cycle, it will not be successful as the main thrust of your chase activity.

To be successful in today's trading conditions you need to be a good communicator, especially in the art of communicating over the 'phone. The telephone is one of the most powerful communication tools ever invented; a confident, professional and relaxed manner is essential if you are to maximise your collection potential.

Every time you approach a collection call you have to believe you are going to collect the debt. Successfully collecting debts by phone is twenty per cent skill and eighty per cent commitment. If you expect to be successful every time you make a collection call, you will probably collect seventy per cent of the debts. If you expect to succeed seventy five per cent of the time, you will probably collect fifty per cent of the debts. If you only expect to be successful fifty per cent of the time, stop what you are doing; clear your desk, and find a new profession. You will never be successful unless you are totally committed. There is no place for the faint-hearted within the credit control profession.

When you communicate face-to-face with someone, you have the advantage of instant visual feedback. Using this feedback you can adjust the level of your conversation to make sure the point you are making is understood. When communicating over the phone this option is not available to you; therefore, it is necessary to develop other skills that enable you to communicate clearly and effectively. The following suggestions will help to improve your telephone technique and your collection response levels.

At this stage it is also worth mentioning that you have to find the language that suits your own personality when speaking to your customers. You need to feel as relaxed as possible when making your collection calls. Only when you have achieved this will you appear truly confident and professional. The following extracts of dialogue are only meant as guidelines, and should not be repeated word for word if you are not comfortable with the language used.

The chase call

Before commencing the chase call, it is always worthwhile trying to find out the name of the person you need to speak to. Psychologists have demonstrated that using someone's name during a conversation works on their psyche, and increases their attention level. This can be used to your advantage by using your debtor's name to raise his attention level during the important stages of your chase call.

Before commencing the call, make sure you have all the available information clearly set out in front of you. Read the account history to refresh your memory, and then use this knowledge to plan your call. Remember, a good collection call doesn't just happen – a lot of thought needs to be put into each call.

By instigating the chase call it is you who has the initiative, and the debtor is the one who needs to do all the quick thinking. Do not give them the opportunity to turn the tables on you by not being adequately prepared. Make sure you have a clear objective in mind and a fallback position beyond which you are not prepared to retreat. Most important of all, never abdicate the initiative to the debtor. Once this has happened you will find it impossible to reach your desired objective. On completion of your call you should summarise the agreements made so that neither party is in any doubt about what is expected of them.

Making a well prepared collection call is not enough. You also need to make it to the right person. Believe me, this is not as stupid as it sounds. To avoid wasting your time make sure you are talking to a decision-maker. It is no use spending five minutes convincing a bought ledger clerk your account should be paid if he does not have the authority to release a cheque.

All too often, credit controllers open a collection call with the statement:

> "Mr Smith, I notice your account still remains unpaid. Could you tell me when you will be sending your cheque?"

On the surface this question seems to be the most logical one to ask. It is certainly what you want to know. However, when you ask the question in this way you are abdicating the initiative to the debtor. You are allowing him to set the time-frame in which to negotiate the payment of your account. For example, the debtor might reply along the lines of:

> *"I never pay this type of account before ninety days".*

Even a good negotiator would find it very difficult to obtain agreement on payment before sixty days. This is because you have allowed the debtor to start the negotiations from a point far in excess of your normal credit terms.

Nine times out of ten, the first call a credit controller makes to a debtor will be a blind call; that is, a call made with no prior knowledge of any disputes or problems on the debt. In these circumstances the call should go something like this:

> *Opening question:* "Mr Smith, I notice your account is overdue for payment. Is there a cheque in the post?"

This question is direct but it is not offensive, and it keeps you in control of the call. If the response to your opening question is,

"I have it here, it has just been signed,"

your *probe question* should be:

"Is that for the full amount of £750?"

It is very important to confirm the amount of the cheque. Otherwise you will often find that the payment you receive will not be for the full debt. If the answer to your probe question is:

"Yes, it's for the full amount of £750",

then your *leading question* should be,

"Mr Smith will that cheque be sent first class post today?"

At the end of this call you should summarise the value of the cheque, the date it is to be sent, and the type of postage to be used. This summary acts as a verbal handshake to cement the agreement.

In the example above, Mr Smith was obviously being very cooperative. As I am sure you are aware, this is not always the case. So let us now look at a situation where Mr Smith is not being quite as helpful.

If you do not get a positive answer to your opening question, and Mr Smith simply replies, "No", then you will need to continue probing Mr Smith's answers until you have the opportunity to open up the conversation. At this stage you must remember that your probe questions should be designed not only to open up the conversation, but also to maintain control of it.

After Mr Smith has replied "No" to your opening question the temptation is to respond along the lines of: "Well, when will you be paying our account, Mr Smith?". As in our first example, this type of question hands the initiative to the debtor. Your first probe question should be:

"Mr Smith, is there a problem with our account?"

If Mr Smith's reply to this question is "No", then you need to probe further. The call would probably follow along these lines:

"If there are no problems with our account, Mr Smith, can you tell me why it has not been paid?"

"I do not know without checking my records."

"I appreciate that, Mr Smith, but as I am on the phone could you just check it out for me?"

It is impossible for you to make a decision regarding Mr Smith's account without being aware of the full facts, and the only way to establish these facts is to continually probe his answers. Eventually you will reach the truth of the matter, which will usually be that the debtor has a cash flow problem. You will learn how to deal with this in a later chapter.

In the second example, the debtor was obviously being difficult. However, it is important that you remember not to lose your temper. Just continue probing until you get to the truth. If you lose your temper you are out of control. If you are out of control you cannot keep command of the conversation or influence its outcome.

Collecting money by using the telephone is a science. You cannot just stumble through call after call to the same debtor without any cohesion or linkage between the calls. Before you start your collection process there is one thing you must remember: if you want to be successful you must follow up your calls progressively, always developing the situation a step further in each call. If you make the same call time after time, without increasing the pressure on the debtor, you will be wasting your time.

Call 1

In your first collection call you should adopt a polite and pleasant attitude. Remember that it is not everyone who is out to take advantage. Some people just need a gentle reminder that the debt is overdue to encourage them to send a cheque. In this call your customer can, and will, expect to be given the benefit of the doubt. The last thing you want to do is to alienate your good customers by reacting in the wrong way to their requests for copy invoices or proof of delivery.

There should not be any real need to get tough in your first call, unless the debtor says something that makes it quite clear he has no intention of paying your account. For example, if your debtor replies: "I only pay my accounts on 90 days so you can take it or leave it", then it will obviously be necessary to apply pressure immediately.

It is possible that by taking a more hostile stance in your first call, you may in fact achieve a higher success rate; however, credit control is not always that simple. If it was only about collecting money, you could stop every customer's account on 30 days and instigate legal action. I am sure your collection rate would go through the roof, but you must remember that every action you take has an equal and opposite reaction. While your collection figures were going through the roof, the sales figures would be falling through the floor.

Credit control is all about balance – collecting debts without alienating the customer. There is no sin in trading a few days' extended credit against future sales. If your first call is being made a few days after the debt is due, it can be no more than a gentle reminder. The success rate for this call will be between 20 and 30 percent; although the figure will vary slightly from industry to industry.

Call 2

The second call you make to your debtor is probably the most important call of the three, and should achieve a 70 per cent success rate when backed up by your first overdue letter. The first thing you need to do is to progress from the first call. You accomplish this progression

51

by taking a firm and assertive stance. Please remember, you do not become assertive by being rude, abrasive, or abusive. There is no place for these stances in effective credit control. Your opening to the second collection call should follow on thus:

> "Mr Smith, I spoke to you last week regarding your overdue account and you promised me a cheque was on its way. We have not received this payment yet, Mr Smith. Is there a problem regarding payment of this account?"

If the debtor replies along the lines of: "I am sure that cheque was sent. I'm a little busy right now, but if you leave it with me I will check it out and get back to you", you now have to decide which way you are going to move. If you just accept what the debtor is saying and wait for him to call back you will not have achieved any progress. To end the call here would be a mistake, as it is very unlikely that the debtor will return your call.

You have now reached the point where you need to be assertive, and this is the area that separates the good credit controllers from the bad. One of the most effective ways to be assertive is to use the technique of turning the debtor's excuse against himself. The beauty of this form of collection is that it is assertive without being aggressive. With this in mind you should progress the call by saying:

> "I appreciate that you are very busy Mr Smith, but could you just check out the payment for me now, as I am on the phone anyway? I do not want to waste any more of your time than I have to."

The debtor would find it hard to argue with this request when it is phrased in this way.

A lot of the excuses used by debtors can be turned to your advantage by using the concept of 'reversing arguments'. Other types of common excuses and their reversing arguments are explained in greater detail in the next chapter.

Even when you do everything right and progress the call in the right way, there are no guarantees that the debtor will definitely send a cheque. However the chances of success are a lot greater than they would have been if you had decided not to progress the call. At least the debtor is aware that you are not going to give up and go away. If you have got that message across, and providing the debtor has the money to pay you, you will probably receive a cheque within a few days.

Call 3

By this stage of your chase cycle the majority of your customers should have cleared their accounts, and any problems such as requests for copy invoices, excuses or grievances should have been dealt with in your previous calls. The debtors who have reached this stage will fall into two categories: those who cannot pay and those who will not pay until they are forced to. Your first problem is to identify which category your debtors fall into, as you need to react differently to each of these problems.

Your third and last call is what I like to call the 'crystal ball call'. In this call you should explain to the debtor the situation as it stands at present, predict his likely future if your account remains unpaid, and – most important of all – make it quite clear to the debtor that this problem is of his own making, and that it is his decision as to which way things go from here.

This third call is unique, because it consists of 100 per cent power. Because of its content it is also the most volatile of the three calls and therefore needs to be handled in a firm, emotionless and professional manner. Many credit controllers feel this is the point where they can really let rip, and blast away indiscriminately with no real cohesion or direction. Nothing could be less productive – there are very few people that you can actually frighten into paying your account.

You persuade your customers to pay you by influencing their decision. You achieve this through reasoned argument, making clear what actions you intend to take to recover your debt, and, if necessary, explaining the consequences the debtor will have to face if you are forced to take this action. You should always end this call by offering the debtor the chance to change his mind and reach a negotiated settlement. If you simply blast away indiscriminately you will not be in control of the conversation. If you are not in control of the conversation you cannot influence the debtor and therefore you will not succeed in encouraging him to pay.

Your opening to the third collection call, then, should go something like this:

> "Mr Smith, I am disappointed to find that you have not responded to our previous requests for payment. Unfortunately you are leaving us no option other than to take legal action against you for the recovery of all moneys owed. I had hoped we could resolve this matter amicably, but it is up to you, Mr Smith. Is this what you want to happen?".

You have now taken the debtor to the point of no return and his reply will give you a strong indication into which category he falls: won't pay or can't pay.

If Mr Smith replies along the lines of,

> *"Everyone else is threatening to sue me. Why should you be any different?",*

this suggests that your debtor has a serious liquidity problem. You should question the debtor further to find out how much money he owes to other creditors, and find out if any of them are taking legal action to recover their debts. You should also ascertain whether your debtor is expecting any money in the near future which will enable him to clear your account. It is always preferable to negotiate a repayment schedule with this type of debtor rather than to sue them. If they really have no money, issuing legal action will not change this fact. Proceeding in this manner will only cost your company money and delay your chance of negotiating a payment proposal by two months or more.

If Mr Smith responds along the lines of:

> *"I don't care if you sue me, you won't get anything",*

then you have to explain the consequences he will suffer if you proceed with legal action. Broadly speaking, these are:

☐ payment of legal costs and statutory interest on top of the original
   debt
☐ loss of credit rating for seven years
☐ the cost of time wasted fighting the legal action
☐ the possibility of being forced into liquidation or bankruptcy.

After you have planted these consequences in Mr Smith's mind,
you should close your call by asking again:

"Is that what you really want to happen, Mr Smith?"

When making your collection calls it is much more productive to
allow the debtor to choose one of several payment options that are
acceptable to you, rather than impose a method of payment on him.
The reason for this is quite simple: when trying to influence people
they are more responsible for, and therefore more likely to adhere to,
ideas they share in, than those imposed upon them.

Throughout all of your collection calls you should make it very
clear to your debtors that any action you are taking is not being taken
because you want to be difficult, but because their actions are leaving
you with no other option. Always try to be conciliatory wherever possible, but never leave the debtor in any doubt that you will take tough
action if necessary to recover the debt.

Once again, remember that during these collection calls you
should avoid losing your temper at all costs. I know that this is easy
to say and difficult to do, but it is very important. There are plenty of
debtors who will be insulting and arrogant on purpose, in an effort to
throw you off balance and make you lose your temper. Once you have
done that they know you have lost the argument. If you lose your
temper you are out of control, and if you are out of control you cannot
influence people.

When you find yourself in this type of situation you should try
mentally to extract yourself from the proceedings and ask yourself:

what is the debtor trying to achieve? Evaluate what his strategy is and decide what you need do to counter it. This type of debtor is using the old American football ploy: the best form of defence is attack. Debtors who follow this strategy are always the ones who have no real excuse for withholding payment of your debt.

Another cardinal sin in these circumstances is to hang up on the debtor. If you do, they have won. It is worth remembering, no matter how abusive they are being, what they are saying is never really personally aimed at you. If the debtor hangs up on you call them back and continue the conversation as if they had never hung up. You should never phone back and say: "I think we were cut off...", you both know that wasn't what happened. It is weak and suggests that you are nervous about continuing the conversation. This type of response will hand the initiative to the debtor.

If the debtor hangs up again do not feel dispirited, simply proceed to the next step in your chase cycle. You cannot expect to be successful all the time, and at least your debtor knows that you are not just going to go away.

Collection letters

I am a strong believer that there is a place in the collection cycle for chase letters. I am the first to admit that letters on their own will not produce much response in the way of payment, but used to complement the three calls listed above they can be an effective tool.

I use two letters in the system I have devised for my company, examples of which are listed below. The first of these letters is used between the second and third phone calls. The second is used after the third phone call prior to handing overdue accounts out to a collection agency.

Our first letter is sent when a debt is approximately 45 days old. We actually have two letters with slightly different text for this stage of our chase cycle. Which one we use is dependant upon our previous conversations with the debtor. The text of these letters is as follows.

Version 1

Dear Mr Smith

Despite our previous requests for payment of your account, it still shows an overdue balance as detailed below.

Our terms and conditions clearly state that all invoices must be paid within thirty days of invoice date.

WE MUST NOW INSIST UPON PAYMENT OF ALL OVERDUE INVOICES WITHIN SEVEN DAYS.

Failure to act on this matter could lead to the suspension of your credit facilities, an interest surcharge of five per cent on the amount due, and ultimately lead to legal action being taken.

We await your remittance by return.

Version 2

Dear Mr Smith

Despite our previous requests for payment, your account still shows an overdue balance as detailed below.

Upon placing advertising with us, you incurred a contractual liability to abide by our terms and conditions of business, which clearly state that all invoices must be paid within thirty days of invoice date.

(contd/...)

(Version 2 contd/...)

As you have not raised any dispute regarding this debt, we are left with no option other than to insist you fulfil your obligation and forward full payment to us within seven days.

Failure to act on this matter will lead to the suspension of your credit facilities, an interest surcharge of five per cent on the amount due, and ultimately lead to legal action being taken.

We await your remittance by return.

The second letter that we send out to our debtors is the final communication they receive from us before we hand their account out to a collection agency. This letter is printed on good quality grey paper and headed: "DEBT RECOVERY ENFORCEMENT DEPARTMENT". The idea behind this letter is for its visual impact as much as its text, to work on the debtor's psyche. Making them realise that matters have now escalated, and that payment should be made before they have to suffer the serious consequences of non payment. The text of this letter is as follows:

Dear Mr Smith

Despite repeated requests for payment of your account, we regret to note that the overdue balance still remains unpaid.

We had hoped that this matter could have been resolved between ourselves, but as your attitude appears to render this impossible, we now intend to instigate third-party

(contd/...)

(Second letter contd/...)

collection action by passing your account out of hand to our Debt Recovery Agency.

Should this course of action fail to bring about the desired results then legal proceedings will be commenced against you without further reference to yourselves.

In accordance with our terms and conditions, upon handing your account out to our collection agency the entire balance of your account, including any current sales, will be deemed due and payable. A five per cent surcharge will also be levied on top of the balance listed below.

This letter regularly achieves a 30 per cent success rate for us. I believe it is a mistake to end a chase letter by saying: "If a cheque has already been sent to clear this account please ignore this letter." To me this is saying one of two things: we are not very good at reconciling payments we receive, or: we are not really serious about the actions we are taking in our letter. Cheques and letters do cross in the post, it's a fact generally accepted by the world of commerce. Whatever you do, don't apologise for it.

Credibility

One of the most important rules in credit management is always to appear credible to your debtor. The debtor must believe that, if you threaten a certain course of action, you will carry it through. This is why you should know exactly what your company's collection policy is, as it is very important that you receive backing for the decisions that you take. If you do not have credibility your collection performance will suffer.

The way you operate your collection system, and the time lag between each phone call, is a matter for yourself and your company. However, there are three factors that must be included in your chase system if you are to achieve your desired results. These are:

☐ a progressive chase cycle
☐ an effective and supportive system

and, last but not least –

☐ establishing credibility.

5

OVERCOMING EXCUSES

Excuses are part of our everyday existence. First encountered in child-hood, well-meant parental evasions dog us for the rest of our lives. As children we have the resolve to argue against them, but not the rea-soning. Somehow, through the process of growing up, most of us acquire the reasoning but manage to lose the resolve... But the habit of making – and accepting – excuses stays with us. It is always easier to accept what someone is saying to you, even if patently false, rather than put your neck on the line and affirm the true logic of the situa-tion. Those people who really succeed in life possess the resolve and the reasoning to overcome excuses, and have their more positive view of reality accepted. If you want to be successful as a credit controller, you will need to do the same.

To succeed in today's business environment, credit controllers not only need to possess the resolution to question what they are being told, they also have to channel it in the correct way to achieve success. The following pages in this chapter will hopefully set you on the road to this success.

Before we look at how to overcome excuses, perhaps we should examine exactly what an excuse is? An excuse is an emotional reac-tion to an event or problem which threatens us. In the world of com-merce this emotional reaction usually manifests itself from three sources: a debtor's fear of not being able to clear all his debts, a debtor's greed, or a passionate dislike for the company or person the debtor is dealing with.

The difficulty in spotting this emotional response comes when the debtor entangles his excuse in false logic which, on the surface, can seem quite feasible. To overcome this false logic you need to soothe the emotion, state the true logic; and, if necessary, apply power. These three steps to overcoming excuses are now discussed in greater detail:

Overcoming false logic

When a debtor makes an excuse for not paying his account, it is your job to turn the tables on him by making the payment of your account his easiest option. To enable you to achieve this you need to overcome the debtor's false logic. At this stage it is important to remember that the debtor's logic may be false, however the emotion behind the logic is real. Therefore you need to overcome the false logic before you can proceed to state the true logic.

You are now entering a crucial phase of the collection cycle; as, when confronted with false logic, the uninitiated credit controller usually reacts in one of two ways. He either starts to argue with the debtor's false logic, or he makes a power play in an effort to resolve the problem quickly. Both of these responses are wrong, and will only lead to further delays in payment.

By arguing with the debtor's false logic, you are allowing him to sidetrack you from your prime objective. If you proceed in this way your call will end up something like this:

(Debtor)"I can't tell you if I have paid your account or not, my books are with my accountant."

"Doesn't your accountant realise that you need constant access to your records? Surely he should be auditing your accounts at your office."

"My accountant works from home. He always has done. This doesn't cause problems with any of my other suppliers."

"I can't believe this has never caused you a problem before. Surely your other suppliers are not willing to wait until you are ready to pay them."

"The other suppliers I deal with seem happy with the way I operate. Most small businesses operate in this way. It is not that uncommon."

In situations like this, the more you argue with the debtor's false logic, the further away you get from securing payment of your debt. If you decide to apply power at this stage, before soothing the emotion and stating the true logic, you will find the results are just as unproductive. In this instance the call will proceed along these lines:

(Debtor)"I can't tell you whether I have paid your debt or not, my books are with my accountant."

"Mr Smith, we both know that I cannot accept that. You must know whether you have paid our account or not."

"I deal with a lot of suppliers, I can't remember all cheques I have raised. Could you remember all the cheques you have received without checking your records?"

By applying the pressure too quickly you are only going to aggravate your debtor. Nobody likes to be called a liar, and at this stage you do not really know whether your debtor is telling the truth or not.

In these situations you have to deal with the debtor's false logic before you can go on to state the true logic. There are no short cuts to obtaining payment if you wish to maintain a business relationship with your debtor. Collecting debts successfully is a combination of quick thinking and a well planned strategy. You obtain payment from your debtor by influencing his thought process. To achieve this you must remain calm and collected.

Stating the true logic

If you want to know whether your debtor really does have a reason for delaying payment, you have to examine his reasoning. You achieve this by asking questions designed to open up the discussion. If carried out correctly your call to Mr Smith should go something like this.

> *(Debtor) "I can't tell you whether I have paid my account or not. My books are with my accountant."*

> "I appreciate your problem Mr Smith; how long will your accountant be working on them?"

> *"I think he will be working on them for the next two weeks."*

> "Two weeks is a long time to be without your records, Mr Smith. I'm sure you must appreciate that we will need payment before then. Is it possible for you to phone your accountant and confirm that our account for £3,000 still remains outstanding?"

> *"That may be possible. If you leave it with me, I'll see what I can find out and get back to you."*

> "Thank you for your co-operation, Mr Smith. I will diarise your account for review on Friday, by which time I should have heard from you."

By approaching the call in this way, you have now obtained a promise from Mr Smith that he will look at your account. You have also made it clear that you are not prepared to wait too long for an answer, and that if Mr Smith does not pay your account within a few days you will be back on the phone chasing him.

The power phase

The power phase is the most dangerous and destructive of all three. It should only be used if all other attempts to make the debtor see reason have failed. Once you have made a power move, you have closed the door on the other options – there is no way back. When applying pressure on the debtor, it is important to make it clear to him that you do not want to take this action, and that what happens next is entirely up to him.

If we follow through our call scenario and assume we have reached Friday, and Mr Smith has not contacted you, your next call has to be a power call. The power call should go something like:

> *(Debtor) "I have not had a chance to speak to my accountant yet. I hope to be speaking to him within the next few days."*

> "Mr Smith when I spoke to you earlier this week you promised me that you would resolve this problem by today. This debt is already approaching 60 days of age Mr Smith, we can't afford to wait any longer for payment."

> *"I'm sorry but I need to check with my accountant before I can pay your account."*

> "Then I must ask you to speak to him, and resolve the matter within the next 48 hours Mr Smith. Otherwise you leave us no option other than to proceed with legal action for the recovery of your debt, costs and statutory interest. It seems so silly that our trading relationship should come to this, Mr Smith. Do we really have to resolve the problem in this way?"

At this stage the call could go one of three ways. First, Mr Smith could admit that he has a cash flow problem. You could then negotiate an instalment proposal to clear the debt (this scenario is discussed later in this chapter.) Secondly, he may remain elusive for the rest of the call, but having had time to weigh the alternatives, he sends the cheque. And lastly, the worst possible outcome, he may decide that he is not prepared to pay his account until he decides it should be paid. In this instance you have no option other than to hand the account out to a third party for collection.

Common excuses

The more experience you gain at overcoming excuses, the more professional your collection call will become. With this in mind I have listed below some of the more common excuses for delayed payment, and how to overcome them.

"No-one is available to sign the cheque."

We do not really know whether this is a case of true or false logic. In order to clarify the situation you should ask the following question.

"When will Mr Smith be returning to the office?"

If he will be back in the office the next day, then the delay seems quite logical. In this case you can ask the bought ledger clerk to leave the cheque on Mr Smith's desk for him to sign when he returns. To add a little urgency to the matter, you can state that you will call Mr Smith tomorrow morning to make sure he has signed the cheque. You should follow up with a call to Mr Smith the next day, stating that you had been promised he would sign the cheque today and you just wanted to make sure that it was in the post.

However, if in answer to your question the bought ledger clerk states that Mr Smith is out of the country for four weeks, then this is obviously an excuse to delay payment of your debt. You should now deal with the emotion and state the true logic by saying:

"I appreciate your problem if Mr Smith is away for four weeks, but I am sure he must have made some provision for paying overdue accounts in his absence".

If the clerk still insists that no provisions have been made for paying overdue accounts, you should continue your questioning along the following lines:

"If Mr Smith has not made any payment provisions, can you tell me who is signing your salary cheques and paying your utility bills?"

If you are lucky the clerk usually admits that Mr Smith did sign some cheques before his departure, but these were only to be used to settle important accounts. (This means he is only to send them out as a last resort, if he has been unable to stall the supplier.) Now that you know Mr Smith has left some signed cheques, you have a window of opportunity to make your power play. Your conversation should continue along the following lines:

(Debtor) "Before his departure Mr Smith did sign a few cheques, but they are only to pay very important accounts that fall due."

"I appreciate what you are saying, but I know that Mr Smith considers our services very important to your company. He will not be pleased if he returns from holiday to find that we have not delivered your supplies, and have in fact suspended your credit facilities."

You have now placed the bought ledger clerk under a lot of pressure by encouraging him to think that if he withholds payment he will be going against the wishes of his boss. By backing up this psychological pressure with the reality of suspended credit facilities, interest surcharge for late payment, and the threat of legal action, you really are piling on the pressure.

"The computer is down."

This is fast becoming the New Age equivalent of "The cheque is in the post." Unfortunately, computer systems do malfunction, therefore the reason for the delay in settling your account could be genuine. Once again, to clarify the situation you need to question the debtor's logic. The call would follow something like:

> *(Debtor) "All of your invoices have been posted on to our computer, but at the present time we are having problems accessing our system. Unfortunately this means we have been unable to print your cheque."*

> "I'm sorry to hear that. It seems we rely so heavily on computers these days. Does your computer usually play up like this?"

> *"It happens three or four times a year."*

> "How long is the system usually down for?"

> *"Sometimes it can take a week or more to repair."*

> "As this is a fairly regular occurrence, I presume that you must have alternative arrangements for paying suppliers' accounts. Is it possible for you to raise a manual cheque for us? We can supply copy invoices if you require them."

If the debtor is genuinely suffering computer problems they will be able and willing to send a manual cheque. If the debtor refuses, they are definitely trying to delay payment; in this case, you have no option other than to apply power to try to secure payment.

"The cheque is in the post."

Right up there with: "Of course I will still love you in the morning, darling", and: "Hello, I'm from head office, I've come to help you", this is one of the Great Lies of all time... Once again, this excuse could be either true or false; however, if you are on the ball it will only buy your debtor an additional 48 hours' credit. Within this time-frame you will know, one way or the other, whether your debtor was telling the truth.

During this call you should work into the conversation the following questions, all of which your debtor should be able to answer if he has sent the cheque:

☐ what is the cheque number?
☐ what was the value of the cheque?
☐ what address was it sent to, and for whose attention?
☐ was it sent first or second class?

Before you finish this call, you should leave the debtor in no doubt that if the cheque does not arrive you will be straight back on the phone wanting to know why – although you would obviously not use that specific phrasing.

"Mr Smith Is not available."

If Mr Smith is unavailable every time you try to contact him, and he never returns your calls, then he is obviously trying to avoid payment. However, all may not be lost. If Mr Smith works for a large company there is one way that you may be able to catch him – you should proceed to phone the company in the normal way, but when you get through to the switchboard, ask for any person in the company other than Mr Smith. When you are put through to this extension you should ask to speak to Mr Smith. Nine times out of ten, the person at the other end of the phone will say: "I'm sorry you have been put through to the wrong extension, if you hold on I'll transfer you." You are then usually transferred direct to Mr Smith and you can speak to him regarding your unpaid account.

In this situation you know that Mr Smith is trying to delay payment, so once you get through to him you should move straight into a power call. This may be the only chance you have of speaking to him, therefore you must leave him in no doubt how serious his delay in payment is, and that you are quite prepared to take tough action if necessary to recover your debt.

Reversing arguments

Debtors do not always try to hide behind false logic. Some believe that the best form of defence is attack. This type of debtor will try to make you feel uncomfortable or unimportant when you call him. He does this in the hope that you will think twice before you call again. In situations like this it is always useful to counter his attack by turning the debtor's excuse on himself.

Reversing arguments are effective because they are assertive without being rude or offensive. You are simply using your debtor's own argument to secure payment. The debtor is then faced with the option of trying to argue against his own logic, or thinking about paying your account. Once you get the debtor thinking positively about paying your account, you are three quarters of the way towards getting paid. I have listed below further examples of how reversing arguments can be used to overcome excuses:

"I'm too busy."

If your debtor replies to your chase call by saying:

"I'm sorry but I am too busy to deal with this problem now",

your reversing argument should be:

"I appreciate how busy you are Mr Smith, I promise I will be brief".

By arguing with this, Mr Smith would actually be saying that he didn't want you to be brief. He would also be wasting his precious time. The quickest way out of this problem would be for Mr Smith to pay your account.

"Can you send a copy invoice."

As you build up a client history, it may become apparent that a particular debtor continually asks for copy invoices before he pays his account. In this case you should deny them any extended credit in the following way.

> *(Debtor) "I am waiting for copy invoices before I can pay your account. I have requested these before."*

> "Is this the only thing that is preventing you paying your account Mr Smith?"

> *"Yes".*

> *"I will fax copies over to you straight away. I presume from what you have said, Mr Smith, that you will have no problem in sending out a cheque tonight for the full value of £750?"*

By turning the tables on Mr Smith, and getting him to agree that the only thing preventing him from paying your account is that he wants a copy of your invoice, he has backed himself into a corner. He now either has to pay your account, or admit that his requests for copy invoices were nothing more than a delaying tactic. As a species we do not like to lose face, so the easiest option for Mr Smith is to pay your account.

"It must have got lost in the post."

Despite all the jokes that circulate around the world of commerce, it is very unusual for the Royal Mail to lose letters. Therefore if someone claims this to be the case, you can be reasonably certain they are stalling for time.

In most cases when a credit controller is faced with this scenario, he asks the debtor when the cheque was sent, the date it was banked, and through which branch it was cashed. All of these questions are valid if you need to trace where the cheque was banked at your end. However, the customer will almost certainly have to contact his bank to answer these questions. Therefore, whether he has sent the cheque or not, you have just given them a further five days before you can contact them again.

Provided your debtor claims the cheque was sent more than a week ago, the question you should be asking is:

"Has the cheque cleared your bank yet?"

The debtor can find the answer to this question within thirty minutes; and what is more, they have to tell the truth. Your debtor cannot say that the cheque has cleared if they have not sent it, because they will not be able to answer all the questions you are now going to ask, i.e. which bank did it clear through, on what date, and – the best one of all – can you supply a copy of both sides of the cheque?

Reversing arguments usually tie the debtor down to the option that makes him take action straight away. They are assertive because you place the onus back on to the debtor. He has to make a decision; and, provided you have played your hand correctly, the simplest option for the debtor should always be to pay your account.

Negotiating payment

We all spend a lot of our waking hours negotiating in some way or other. In fact, I would go as far as to say that life is just one continuous negotiation. Some of us are good at it and some of us are not, but one thing is certain: very few of us ever give it much thought.

Negotiation can be a very complex matter, therefore in this chapter I have simply attempted to supply you with a few tips that may be of use when negotiating with debtors who have cash flow problems.

Before entering into negotiations there are two requirements that you must fulfil: first, you should make sure you are talking to a decision-maker. As the name suggests, a decision-maker is someone who can make a decision as to how and when you will be paid. This will usually be one of the following: director, partner, proprietor or financial controller.

Having reached the decision-maker, you now need to know whether the debtor is suffering a short-term cash flow problem, or has no money at all. You should ask the following questions to help clarify the situation.

> "Mr Smith, will you be able to clear your account in full when you receive money owed to you?"

If the debtor replies along the lines of:

> *"We are expecting some large cheques within the next two weeks – once we have received these we will be able to clear your account",*

then, provided the debtor is telling you the truth (your past trading history with the debtor will help you to assess this), you should be paid within a few weeks.

If the debtor replies along the lines of:

> *"We are expecting some money within the next few weeks and at this stage we should be able to clear part of your account",*

then the debtor obviously has a more serious cash flow problem. Having established that this is the case, you now need to find out how serious the problem is, and if the debtor is likely to be around long enough to enter into an instalment agreement. You should ask:

"How many other creditors do you owe money to Mr Smith, and are any of them taking legal action to recover their debts?"

If Mr Smith states that he owes money to four large suppliers, and has come to an agreement with them to settle their debts by monthly instalments, then you should enter into negotiation regarding the payment of your debt.

If on the other hand Mr Smith states that he owes money to a number of creditors and three of these are taking legal action against him, your chances of obtaining payment through negotiation are pretty slim. No matter what Mr Smith says, he will pay the people taking legal action against him first. After all, they are the ones that are shouting the loudest. If your debt is of a reasonable size I would suggest your only hope of payment is to take legal action yourself.

The second requirement is, when trying to asses which category your debtor falls into, you need to take into account the amount of money he owes. If your debtor owes you one hundred pounds, and wants to clear it over three months this is not a cash flow problem, it is a no-money problem...

Having obtained as much financial information from the debtor as possible, you are now ready to start negotiating. Before you start, you should always have a figure in mind that you require as a down payment. If you need to concede anything during the negotiation it is advisable to give way on the number of instalment payments, not the amount you require as a down payment. The down payment is cash in the bank, the promise of instalment payments is pure conjecture until they happen. For the following example, I am going to accept a figure of £5000 as a down payment.

You should start the negotiations by asking Mr Smith:

"How do you plan to pay this debt?"

This forces the debtor to make a commitment to discuss the situation, and it is here that the negotiations are thrown open.

The debtor's answer will usually follow along the lines of:

"How much are you willing to accept?"

In reply you should always state:

"We will accept the full amount Mr Smith, but if you could send us seven thousand now it would be a start."

By asking for £7,000 you have made it clear to the debtor that you want a substantial figure as a down-payment. You have also allowed yourself a reasonable amount of leeway over your acceptable down payment figure, in case the debtor tries to trade down your offer.

Let us presume that you finally agree on a down payment of £5,000. In your debtor's eyes you have made a concession of £2,000 on your original request, therefore you are entitled to trade that concession for something you want. One of the golden rules of negotiating is that you always trade your concessions. Having agreed on the down payment figure, your next question should be:

"Can we expect the remaining £5,000 next month?"

The debtor will no doubt try to clear the balance over a number of instalments. Having agreed on a number you can both live with, it is now time to trade the concession you earned by reducing your down payment figure. This concession should be traded for post dated cheques to cover the instalment payments.

Post dated cheques may be worthless until they are honoured by the debtor's bank, however they do have one important purpose: by encouraging the debtor to give you post dated cheques, you have coerced him into making a psychological commitment to clear your debt. Psychologists have stated that the debtor will feel a far greater need to honour this commitment than any verbal agreement made to send instalment payments.

The above example is fine if the debtor is cooperating with you, however we all know that this is not always the case. When you encounter a debtor who is not being very cooperative, you need to change your strategy slightly.

The initial stages of this call will be the same as the example above; however, when you reach the point where you ask the debtor:

"How do you plan to clear this debt?",

the debtor may answer by saying:

"I can pay you one hundred pounds a month."

This is an absurd figure and you should not place yourself in a position where you even so much as discuss it. Even if the debtor was true to his word it would take him over eight years to clear his account.

When you are faced with this situation you have two basic choices: option one is where you make a power play to try and force the debtor to capitulate. Option two is where you defer making a decision on his offer by removing yourselves from the negotiation, saying:

"I am sorry Mr Smith I am not even allowed to discuss an offer of that level. Our company policy in these matters is...", etc.

When the debtor realises that you have no intention of discussing his offer the usual response is:

"Well, how much will you accept then?"

You are now back in control and can reply:

"We need payment of the full amount but we will accept £5,000 now as a down payment."

Negotiating is not easy. It takes skill and confidence, which will only come with practice. You will not always be able to conclude successful negotiations. Some of the debtors you call will be lost causes who, when they say they have no money, actually have no money. However, there are a number of debtors who will continue to trade quite happily for many years after you have written off their debts as bad. These debtors will be very good at giving the impression they are in a grave financial state when in fact they have plenty of money to clear your account. It is surprising how, when push comes to shove, they can manage to lay their hands on some money.

I remember one case a few years ago where a debtor owed my company £3,000. It turned out that he was a bankrupt, whose limited company had crashed owing approximately £200,000. He was now supposedly operating as a consultant for an identical business owned by his wife. Given that the situation seemed fairly hopeless, it was agreed to accept payments of £200 a month to clear the debt. After a few months the payments ceased, our debtor claiming poverty.

Unfortunately for this debtor, he lived only a few minutes' drive from my home, so it was not difficult for me to find out exactly what type of 'abject poverty' he was living in. His wife, who supposedly owned the business, also owned the house – which had been transferred into her name the day before the husband's bankruptcy hearing. This property could only be described as a mansion; there were also two brand new cars in the drive, belonging to our debtor's wife... If this was abject poverty, I could certainly do with some of it.

Having finished my stint as agent 003-and-a-bit, I returned to work and issued legal action against our debtor's wife (the supposed owner of the business). After obtaining judgement, I issued bankruptcy proceedings against her in the hope that I could force our debtor's hand. Not surprisingly he was none too pleased about this; however, within a few days he found the money to clear our debt, costs, and statutory interest.

No matter how hopeless the situation may seem, it is always worth trying to negotiate with the debtor. You never know what sources of money you may unearth.

6

INFLUENCING YOUR DEBTORS' PAYMENT HABITS

The aim of every credit controller should be to collect his company's debts efficiently and without the loss of customer goodwill. The most effective and least confrontational way for you to achieve this is by influencing your debtors' payment habits. There are basically two ways in which you can achieve this when making a collection call: the first is through the language you use during the call, and the second is through the actual content of the call.

Great care should be given to the language you use during your chase calls. If you use language that puts your debtor on the defensive, or worse still turns him off altogether, you are seriously affecting the impact of the second stage of your influencing strategy. The content of your call may be influential and well thought out, however this will be totally ineffectual if you have caused your debtor to switch off through the choice of language used.

You should always remember that people can be alienated as easily as they can be influenced. The right thing said in the wrong way can lead to confrontation, lost objectives, and – more importantly – the loss of a valued customer.

In the past, debtors felt a personal need to honour their debts. Unfortunately, the two recessions of the 'eighties put paid to this way of thinking. Today, you will have to manipulate your debtor's commercial need to pay you, if you are going to influence his payment habit. Simply bringing to your debtor's attention the fact that his account is overdue will no longer be enough to secure payment. Your debtor is already aware that he owes you money and will only pay you when it suits him to do so. In these cases your objective is to make your debtor want to pay your account, when you want it paid.

The least confrontational way to achieve this is by applying influence over your debtor's payment habits. It sounds simple, doesn't it? Unfortunately it is not quite that simple.

Despite what you may be told in training videos there is no such thing as a uniform debtor. Mr Average Debtor is a mythical character, right up there with King Arthur and the Boggie... In all honesty you are more likely to find Nessy the Loch Ness monster, than a typical debtor. So, do not waste your time trying to perfect the catch-all collection strategy, because it does not exist. Each of your debtors is an individual, and you will need to find more than one way to influence him. The real difficulty comes in finding the right influencing factor for each debtor.

Some of your debtors will need to be cajoled into paying their account, while with others you will need to take a firm line right from your first call. The key in these circumstances is to get to know your debtors and how to satisfy their needs, while meeting your objectives. Once you have managed to achieve this you will be able to make all your collection calls more effective.

Before you start your chase call there is one thing you need to understand: your debtor is interested only in his needs, he has no interest whatsoever in your needs. When making your call, try to avoid using phrases such as: "We want your cheque today", "We need your cheque today","We must have your cheque by Wednesday at the latest." These type of statements are only associated with your needs, not those of your debtor.

When making your collection call you should always hold this thought in your mind: "If you are to be successful in collecting your debt, you need to satisfy your debtor's needs while meeting your own objectives".

Making the call

As stated earlier, before you can influence a debtor's payment pattern you need to know what his needs are. The only way to obtain this information is to converse with the debtor, listen to his response from which you can assess his needs, and then select the correct influencing factor to satisfy them.

If your debtor is the type of customer who will only take action when he thinks things are getting serious, then you will need to be assertive right from the start if you are to influence him. From your first phone call you will need to make it very clear what you expect from him, placing the emphasis on the consequences he will suffer if he does not play ball.

If on the other hand your debtor is a little less decisive, you should put more emphasise on persuading him to pay your account. You achieve this by putting your case forward in its strongest form, while backing up your argument with any relevant facts and figures. If during your conversation the debtor comes up with a compromise, do not ignore it. You should accept the idea and develop it if necessary to suit your objectives. But remember, do not develop the idea so far that it no longer fulfils your debtor's requirements. If it no longer satisfies his needs he will not go along with it.

Finally, when making the call remember to remain positive at all times. Not only in your ideas but also the language you use. If you can convince your debtor that you want to find a positive solution that will be of benefit to everyone, he is much more likely to keep an open mind and react to your suggestions in a positive manner.

Matching the correct influencing factor

As you speak to your debtor you need to analyse his response so that you can pinpoint his specific need. Having pinpointed his need you can then select the correct influencing factor to satisfy it. This skill can only be obtained through practice; however, to help guide you in the right direction I have listed below some of the more common influencing factors, and when and how they should be used.

Suspension Of Credit

This is probably the first influencing factor that comes to mind when credit controllers start to think about influencing their debtors' payment patterns. In fact, I would go as far as to say that in fifty per cent of the credit control departments in this country, it is probably the only influencing factor used. It is standard policy for most credit control departments to send out standard chase letters as part of their collection cycle. These letters usually state that the non-payment of your debt will result in the suspension of credit facilities, and are sent to all overdue debtors, regardless of whether they are still trading with the company or not. This type of blanket usage tends to be unproductive, and has led to a loss of impact for this influencing factor.

In truth, the suspension of credit can only, and will only, work on customers who use your company on a regular and continuous basis. It will have absolutely no effect on debtors who have used your company on a one-off basis, or those who have reached the end of their trading relationship with you. These debtors do not have a need to purchase any further goods or services from your company, therefore you cannot influence their payment habits by suspending credit facilities they no longer wish to use.

The other side of the equation is the debtor who trades on a regular basis with your company, where the profitability or success of his business is linked to this trading relationship. This debtor has a very strong need for your goods or services, therefore threatening to suspend his credit facilities is a powerful influencing factor.

It is possible that some of your debtors will have more than one need to fulfil. In these circumstances you should always work on the greatest need. The greater the debtor's need, the greater the power of the influencing factor, and the greater the level of your success.

Credit Rating

Credit rating can be used as either a positive or negative influencing factor, but the way in which you use it will be dependent on your trading relationship with your debtor. For example, if your debtor uses your company on a regular basis for trade references, he will have a need for you to report positively on his trading performance. This can become a fairly powerful need which you can exploit to speed up payment of your own account.

If in these circumstances Mr Smith's payment performance starts to decline, you should remind him that unless your account is paid within a reasonable time-frame, it will affect the trade references you give on his behalf. By using the influencing factor in this way you are satisfying Mr Smith's need for a good trade reference, linking it to your objective of getting Mr Smith to pay his account on time.

The negative influencing factor can be used on debtors who do not consider the payment of your debt to be a priority. This problem is fairly common within the industry that I work in. For example, a debtor may run a series of advertisements in one of our publications. Having received the benefit of the advertising, and not intending to use our services again in the near future, the debtor does not feel any need to give our account priority.

This type of debtor may feel he has no immediate need for your services and therefore no need to pay your account quickly. However, he will undoubtedly have suppliers who are important to him, both now and in the future. Therefore, in this scenario I would suggest you try to influence the debtor in the following way:

> "I appreciate that payment of our account may not be your number one priority, however I feel I should inform you that we do supply payment information to all the leading business information companies. Any delay in the payment of our account, Mr Smith, could affect the credit rating they give your company."

By using the credit rating factor in its negative form, you are feeding on the debtor's need to maintain a good credit rating to achieve your objective of securing payment of your account. If your debtor already has a bad credit rating then this influencing factor is not going to work. In this scenario the only option left open to you is the threat of legal action.

To get you off their backs

This influencing factor will only work on debtors who are too busy to waste time arguing with you over payment of their account. It will not be effective on large or medium-sized companies, who have dedicated accounts payable departments. Bought ledger clerks spend the whole of their day dealing with people chasing them for payment. It is the reason they are employed, and if you are not on the phone chasing them, someone else will be.

This influencing factor is designed for small businesses who do not have an accounts department. With this type of debtor the person you are talking to will almost certainly be the proprietor of the business. As such, his time could be spent more productively on other activities rather than dealing with you.

This type of debtor is quite often aggressive in his response when you first start your chase cycle. He reacts in this way in the hope that he can deter you from calling again. However, once he realises that you are persistent, the easiest option for him is to pay your account and get you off his back. One word of warning: make sure you do not cross that thin line between persistence and harassment – recognise that small businesses often have trouble obtaining payment from their own customers in turn.

Credit limit

This influencing factor can only work on a debtor who depends on you supplying goods or services for the continuation of his business. In these circumstances, the amount of credit offered to your debtor is a lifeline to him and, hence, a very powerful influencing factor.

As this debtor is reliant on your goods or services he will be a regular customer; and, as such, will also be susceptible to the 'suspension of credit' influencing factor. In most cases it is this route that companies will follow when trying to get him to pay his account. However, trying to influence your debtor's payment habits by using credit limits has two important advantages in its favour:

First, by using the credit limit influencing factor, you will maintain a more harmonious trading relationship with your debtor. Just because your debtor has reached his credit limit it does not mean he has done anything wrong, therefore the debtor should not become defensive when he is advised of the situation. Secondly, as you are not accusing the debtor of any wrong doing, you can use this influencing factor earlier in your chase cycle and hopefully speed up payment of your account. If this approach is unsuccessful, you still have the option of moving to the 'suspension of credit' factor, to induce payment.

Increased costs

This influencing factor can be used on any of your debtors, but will be most effective against those who are cash-managing your money. The 'increased costs' factor has two modes of operation: on the positive side, you can offer your customers a prompt payment discount. This will be appealing to those debtors who have the money to clear your account but are withholding payment to improve their own trading position. Unfortunately, it will not work on debtors who do not have the necessary cash flow to pay your account on time.

The second way this influencing factor can be used is in the form of a penal charge for late payment, which should be incorporated in your terms and conditions of sale. This charge is often invoked at the stage where you have to hand your debtor's account out to a third party for collection. This action will increase your collection costs, and there is no reason why the charge should not be passed on to your debtor. If you fail to penalise your debtor in some way once he has reached this stage, then you are not giving him an incentive to pay his account on time in the future.

You must remember that this influencing factor has to be used on a decision-maker; it will not work on bought ledger clerks. They have very little influence over when your account is paid and even less interest in any additional costs that their company may have to pay.

Legal action

The thought of having to go to court can frighten debtors who have no real reason for withholding payment of your account. It also tends to concentrate their mind on the problem at hand; and, as such, I suppose this action can be classed as an influencing factor. However, I personally see it as an end result when all other forms of influence have failed. If you have not obtained payment by this stage, you can be fairly certain that your debtor either has no money to pay you, or intends to make you fight very hard to get your hands on it. If he is really determined and plays the legal system to his full advantage, he could make you wait anything up to eighteen months before you see your money.

If you are using a three-call chase cycle, all of the influencing factors, with the exception of the threat of legal action, should be incorporated into your second call. The threat of legal action should only be used as a last resort and therefore encompassed within your last chase call.

As previously stated, there is no collection procedure in existence that is a perfect panacea; the use of influencing factors is no exception. However, provided your debtor does intend to pay your account at some stage, the use of influencing factors will speed up the point at which you receive payment.

Learning to match the right influencing factor to the right debtor will only come with experience. It will appear difficult at first, but persevere with it. Once you have learned to master this strategy, it will definitely reduce the length of time it takes you to recover your debts. I have included a quick reference table at the end of this chapter to help clarify the most common influencing factors, and the type of debtor they will be most effective against.

If your debtors are more devious about paying their accounts, then the use of influencing factors may not be the most effective collection strategy to use. In this instance it may be more beneficial to use the collection strategy of 'overcoming excuses' as detailed earlier in this book.

The role of the credit controller is definitely changing. If the modern day credit controller is to be successful he needs to be more multidirectional in his approach to collecting overdue debts. No matter what type of debtor you are dealing with, somewhere in the preceding three chapters you will find the key to unlock their personal door to payment. The only exception to this is the debtor who is basically a crook and never had any intention of paying your account. Fortunately these debtors are few and far between.

Influencing Factors – Quick Reference Guide

Influencing factor	Type of debtor it works on
Suspension of credit	Any debtor who buys your goods or services on a regular or continuous basis
Credit Rating: **- Positive**	Debtor who uses your company for trade references.
- Negative	Debtor who doesn't see your goods or services as important to him.
Get you off their backs	Small business where time would be better spent on other priorities.
Credit limit	Debtor who depends on your goods or services for the continued existence and growth of their business.
Increased costs	Useful against all debtors, through cash discounts for prompt payment or surcharges for slow payment. (Most effective against debtors who are cash-managing your money.)
Legal Action	The final action to be used against debtors when all other options

---

7

COLLECTION AGENCIES AND SOLICITORS

No matter how professional or effective a credit control department is, there will always be some debts that it will be unable to collect. These debtors will be made up of customers who cannot afford to pay their debt, and those who will not pay until they are forced to. Whether you are dealing with the 'Can't pays' or the 'Won't pays', you have now reached the point where you need to hand the account out to a third party for collection. But who do you choose to carry on the chase cycle?

Many companies feel that using a collection agency would be of little benefit. They believe that, if their credit controllers have carried out their job correctly, the collection agency would have very little extra impact on their uncollected debts. I have to say here and now that this is not the case: a letter or phone call from a collection agency has a proven psychological effect on the debtor.

By handing your unpaid accounts out for third party collection, you have escalated the situation. Probably for the first time in your chase cycle, your debtor feels threatened. Things are now getting serious and you are forcing him to respond in one form or another. Of course, this will not enable the debtor who can't pay to find, suddenly, the resources he needs to clear your debt; but it will focus his mind on the problem. More often than not, though, it leads to your debt being cleared through instalment payments.

Once the in-house collection cycle has been completed, I always prefer to move to a collection agency for the next level of contact, rather than proceed directly to legal action. I fully accept that letters from a solicitor or collection agency will have broadly the same psychological impact; however, a collection agency will only charge for its services if it is successful in collecting the debt, while a solicitor will charge you for a collection letter regardless of whether he is successful or not. You should also remember that legal firms make their money from suing people – no matter what their advertisements claim, they do not make money from, and are not interested in, collecting debts for a fee of £1.50 a time.

If a collection agency is performing well, it should be able to collect seventy to eighty per cent of the accounts handed out to it, provided the debts are clean (free from queries, and of a reasonable age). Let us now take a detailed look at how collection agencies and solicitors operate when collecting your debts:

The collection agency

Over the last decade, the quality of service offered by collection agencies has had to evolve to keep pace with the growth in importance of the credit control function. Twenty years ago most collection agencies used to sell their services by way of a voucher system, that required payment for a whole year's service in advance. This type of system was based around a three-letter chase cycle; no direct contact was made with the debtor, which severely hampered their success rate.

The services offered by today's collection agencies are vastly different. First and foremost, payment is made on results. If the agency do not collect the debt, they do not get paid. This tends to make them a little more eager to succeed. Secondly, their chase cycle will consist of letter and phone contact, which results in the maximum amount of pressure being exerted on the debtor. Despite this improvement you still need to be wary of whom you are dealing with.

Some of today's less reputable agencies are enticing customers to use their services through intensive advertising campaigns that depict a very low-cost collection service. Unfortunately, the reality is that the collection system is designed to be totally ineffective, and is just a front for what is a very expensive and fairly inept legal collection service. This type of marketing is not illegal, but it is amoral. They are feeding on the desire that exists in every one of us to get something for nothing. The sad truth in this game is that if you pay peanuts, you get monkeys.

At this point I should make it clear that I am not saying every company that offers competitive prices is on the make; however you should ensure that you know what type of service you are getting for your money, and how quickly the service proceeds to legal action.

When choosing a collection agency, it is always worthwhile taking up independent references from other companies which have used them. Any reputable agency will be willing to give you a list of clients whom you can approach. It will also be worth while making sure that the agency is licensed for debt collection under the Consumer Credit Act 1974, and also registered with the Office of Fair Trading.

Having chosen to use a collection agency, you now have to decide at which stage in your chase cycle you want to bring in its services. I believe if you want to get the most out of a collection agency you should use them while the debt is still collectable. I hand out accounts at approximately 65 days, by which time we have completed our in-house chase cycle and the agency's involvement can still have the maximum impact. At 65 days the debts will still be very collectable and the agency should produce good results.

Even after handing your accounts to the collection agency, you should make sure you still maintain control of them. You should not allow your accounts to remain with the agency for too long, so make sure you set the time-frame for the agency's chase cycle. A typical time-frame would be: day one, send first letter. Day four, make first phone call. Day eleven, make second phone call. Day eighteen, send final application threatening legal action. Day twenty five, refer to client for permission to issue legal proceedings.

After their final application, the agency should always refer back to you for authorisation before proceeding with legal action. Once you proceed with legal action your costs will start to rise fairly rapidly.

Choosing the right collection agency for your company is a personal matter. You are the best judge as to which one will meet your company's needs; however I would recommend that you:

☐ use an agency that operates on a 'no collection, no fee' basis.
☐ Don't agree to any close out or file charges. These are only a back door way of obtaining money for admin charges.
☐ Constantly monitor your collection agency's results. A strike rate of at least 70 per cent should be obtained.
☐ Make sure you set the collection time frame for the agency to work to.
☐ Make sure all payments made to the agency are forwarded to you and not banked by the agency. On the odd occasion when the agency has to bank your cheque, make sure it is paid into a client account. It is then safe if anything happens to the agency.
☐ Use an agency that has phone contact with the debtor and not one that just uses a letter chase cycle.
☐ Make sure the agency is registered with the Office of Fair Trading, and licensed for debt collection under the Consumer Credit Act 1974.

The collection rates charged by agencies are by their very nature index-linked, and therefore do not need to be increased. As inflation causes the cost of your goods or services to rise, the value of your debts sent to the collection agency will also increase. This in turn leads to an increase in the agency's commission. The example of Cogg & Co. Ltd shows this trend in action. For this, I have assumed that:

☐ inflation in 1994 ran at 4%
☐ the cost of widgets in Jan 1994 = £10.00
☐ the cost of widgets in Jan 1995 = £10.00 + 4% inflation = £10.40

In January 1994, Cogg & Co. purchased 1,000 widgets at a cost of £10,000. In 1995, Cogg & Co. purchased a further 1,000 widgets at the inflation increased price of £10,400. On both occasions the debt is sent out to a collection agency to be recovered. The collection commission charged by the agency is 4%, therefore the collection cost for the 1,000 widgets sold in 1994 was £400 (i.e., £10,000 x 4% = £400). The collection cost for the 1,000 widgets sold in 1995 will be £416 (i.e., £10,400 x 4% = £416). The £16 increase in collection commission year-on-year is equivalent to the 4% rise in the level of inflation.

If a collection agency does try to increase its charges, it can only be for one of the following reasons:

☐ The agency initially set their collection charges at an uneconomic level to obtain your business. Now having obtained your commitment they need to increase their charges to make your business profitable.

☐ They decide it is worthwhile taking the risk of increasing their charges to enable them to increase their profits, while hoping they do not lose too many clients.

☐ The collection agency is not controlling its own costs properly, and tries to get its customers to pay for its inefficiency.

☐ The collection agency is not producing very good collection results and needs to increase its charges to stay in business.

Measuring performance

Having chosen the collection agency that best suits your company's needs, the next step is to monitor its performance. This is probably best done on a monthly basis, and will take two forms: firstly, you need to measure the number of accounts you are handing out to the agency. Secondly, you need to measure the collection performance of the agency itself. Remember, having accounts grow old in the agency's hands, is just as costly as having them grow old in yours.

Keeping a check on the level of debt being passed to the collection agency is very important. It is a good measure of how well your in-house collection system is working. Despite its importance, you would be surprised how many companies measure this performance in the wrong way. In many cases you will find companies measuring nothing more than the change in the total agency debt, month-on-month. If this figure appears to rise for a few consecutive months, you will be asked what is going wrong with your in-house collection procedure. However, if the figure reduces for a few consecutive months, you are told what a great job you are doing.

The truth of the matter is that, unless your sales revenue remains static month-on-month, measuring the level of debts passed to your collection agency tells you absolutely nothing about your in-house collection performance. The only measure that will show a clear picture of your in-house collection performance and agency debt-to-sales ratio is the plotting of your company's accumulated sales figure against its accumulated agency debt figure. This may sound a little complicated but, believe me, you do not have to be a mathematical genius to understand the concept.

The clearest way to illustrate this measurement is to plot your company's accumulated sales and agency debt figures on the same graph. If nothing is changing month-on-month, the two lines will remain parallel to each other. If the amount of debt at the agency is increasing, but at a slower rate than the monthly sales revenue (i.e., your in-house collection results are improving, and less debt as a percentage of sales is being sent to the agency), the two lines will move apart. If the opposite is happening and the amount of debt at the agency is growing at a faster rate than the monthly sales revenue (i.e., your in-house collection performance is declining and more debts as a percentage of sales are being handed to the agency), the two lines will move together.

There is one last thing you need to consider before looking at the graphs below, which is that debts are not handed to the agency as soon as they are generated. Therefore, when measuring collection agency debt against sales, you need to compare the agency debt against the relevant sales month. For example, if you hand debts out to a collection agency on 60 days, the debts sent to the agency in June will have been generated from the sales made in April. Therefore you need to measure June's collection agency debts against April's sales figures.

In the following examples we are going to presume that all three companies hand their debts out to a collection agency on 60 days.

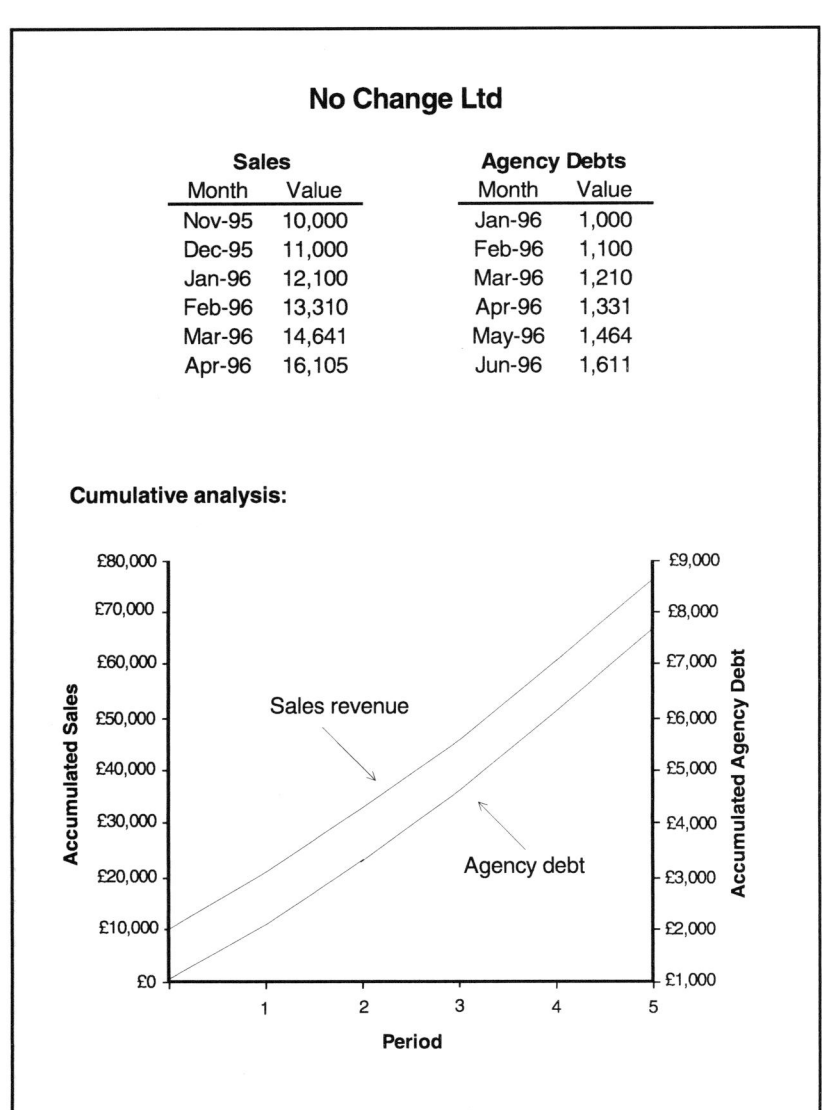

Fig. 7:1 Collection Agency analysis for No Change Ltd

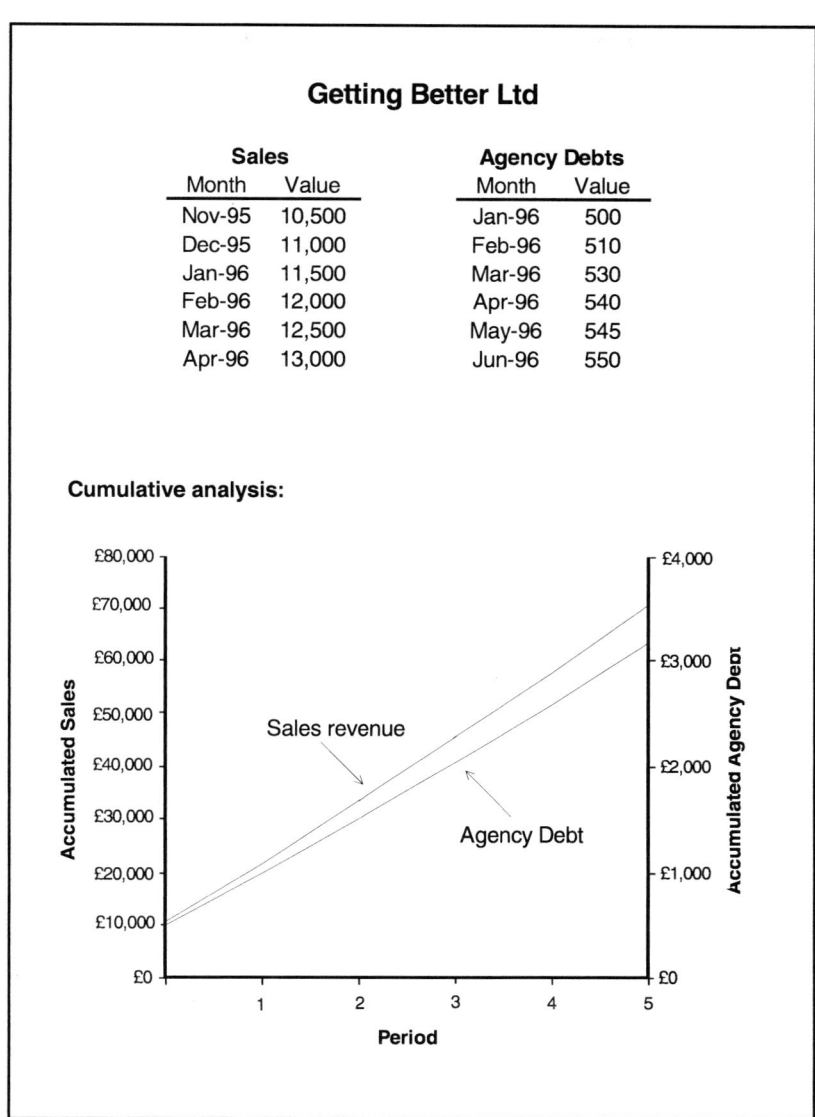

Getting Better Ltd

Sales			Agency Debts	
Month	Value		Month	Value
Nov-95	10,500		Jan-96	500
Dec-95	11,000		Feb-96	510
Jan-96	11,500		Mar-96	530
Feb-96	12,000		Apr-96	540
Mar-96	12,500		May-96	545
Apr-96	13,000		Jun-96	550

Cumulative analysis:

Fig. 7:2 Collection Agency analysis for Getting Better Ltd

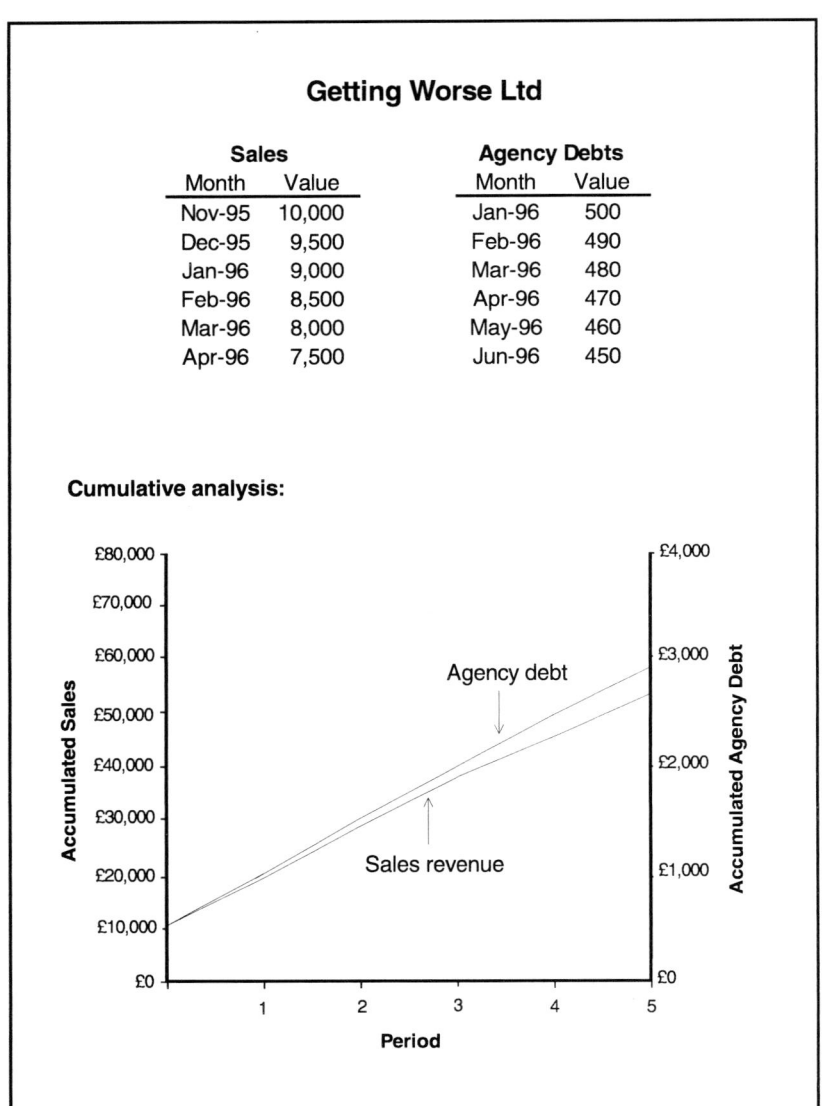

Getting Worse Ltd

Sales			Agency Debts	
Month	Value		Month	Value
Nov-95	10,000		Jan-96	500
Dec-95	9,500		Feb-96	490
Jan-96	9,000		Mar-96	480
Feb-96	8,500		Apr-96	470
Mar-96	8,000		May-96	460
Apr-96	7,500		Jun-96	450

Cumulative analysis:

Fig. 7:3 Collection Agency analysis for Getting Worse Ltd.

If you looked purely at the agency debt figures for No Change Ltd, the only assumption you could make is that the level of agency debt is increasing. This leads people to assume that the in-house debt collection process is not operating efficiently. However, when you look at the complete picture, you can see that the level of debts with the agency is in fact increasing at the same rate as the sales revenue. Therefore the actual in-house collection performance has not changed at all, as can be seen in *fig. 7:1*.

In the example for Getting Better Ltd, shown in *fig. 7:2*, the debts with the collection agency are again increasing month-on-month. However, this time they are increasing at a slower rate than the increase in sales revenue. Once again, if we simply looked at the agency debt figures, we would conclude that the in-house collection system is not being run efficiently. But when we look at the complete picture it shows the exact opposite: the level of debt being passed out to an agency as a percentage of sales is reducing, which means that the in-house collection system is improving.

In the final example for Getting Worse Ltd, shown in *fig. 7:3*, the debt at the agency is reducing, but at a slower rate than the decline in sales revenue. Once again, simply by looking at the level of agency debt you would get a distorted picture, as it would appear that the in-house collection performance was improving when, in fact, the exact opposite would be happening.

This is an important concept to grasp; so, at the risk of boring you, I will repeat it one more time: the level of debt being handed out to the collection agency can only be accurately assessed by measuring the accumulated sales against the accumulated agency debt figure. Looking at the collection agency debt as a figure on its own, or as a percentage of outstanding sales, which is another popular measure, will tell you absolutely nothing.

You will be glad to know that the measurement of the collection agency's performance, by comparison, is quite straightforward. The golden rule here is to measure your agency's performance by the number of accounts collected, and not the value of debt collected. The latter can easily be distorted if a couple of large value debts are handed out to the agency. The other thing you need to remember is to deduct any accounts you may have closed out on; or those which, as a result of the agency's actions, have been queried with the sales department. If you do not make these adjustments you will seriously distort the agency's success rate. The example in *fig. 7:4*, shows how I monitor the success rate of the agency I use.

As you can see from *fig. 7:4*, I break down the percentage of debts placed legal, as well as the percentage written off. This type of information should be easy to extract from your collection agency report and is priceless when it comes to reporting to senior management. As I stated earlier, the measurement of the collection agency's performance really is quite simple; the only thing you need to consider now, is at what stage you measure its performance.

C.T.C.A. Collection Agency

Total amounts handed out in June	152
Less amounts closed out	(17)
Less accounts in query	(21)
Total of active accounts	**114**
Accounts paid in full	86
Accounts placed legal	26
Accounts to be written off	2
Accounts still being chased	0
Total	**114**
Percentage of accounts paid	75%
Percentage of accounts placed legal	23%
Percentage of accounts written off	2%

Fig. 7:4 Collection Agency performance analysis.

I always compile my reports at the end of the month following the month the debts were handed to the agency, e.g., accounts handed to the agency during June will be reviewed at the end of July. As I hand accounts out to the agency every week, if I measured their results at the end of June, the agency would only have an average of 17.5 days to collect the debt. As the collection procedure I have asked them to follow takes approximately 30 days to complete, it would be unfair to judge their performance at 17.5 days. By reviewing their performance at the end of July, an average of 45 days from handing the account out to them, I receive a more accurate analysis of their performance.

Setting up an in-house collection agency

During the last recession, as a way of trying to cut collection costs, some companies looked at setting up their own in-house collection agencies. But how useful are in-house collection agencies? How difficult are they to set up, and are they cost-effective?

The idea of setting up an in-house collection agency is very appealing. It is nice to know that you can always keep a hands-on approach with your debtors throughout the entire chase cycle. However, an in-house collection agency may not always be the most economical way of collecting your debts. This will depend on the size of your company, and the number and value of accounts you hand out to the collection agency each month.

If this type of set-up is going to be successful, it is imperative you convince your debtors that they are being contacted by a bona fide collection agency. If you fail to create this illusion you will not supply the stimulus needed to create the correct psychological reaction in your debtor's mind. Without this reaction, you will not achieve the required levels of collection.

Let us look at two companies, both operating in London and using the same collection agency. For this example we will assume that the collection agency are successful in collecting 85 per cent of all debts handed out to them, which is not an unrealistic figure.

	Worthwhile Ltd	Notsogood Ltd
Outside collection agency:		
Accounts	200	80
Average value	£700	£500
Average cost of collection	4%	4%
Debts handed out per annum	£1,680,000	£480,000
Revenue collected per annum	£1,428,000	£408,000
Costs incurred per annum	£57,120	£16,320
In-house collection agency:		
Salary senior credit conrtoller	£17,000	£17,000
Salary junior credit controller	£14,000	£14,000
Employment costs	£6,200	£6,200
Holdiday cover	£1,400	£1,400
Telephone costs	£2,500	£1,000
Stationery	£500	£200
Postage	£864	£346
Total costs incurred per annum	£42,464	£40,146
Comparison:		
Outside agency costs	£57,120	£16,320
Less in-house agency costs	-£42,464	-£40,146
Gain/(loss) using outside agency	£14,565	-£23,826

Fig. 7:5 Comparison of independent & in-house collection agencies

From the figures listed above, it is quite clear that the number of accounts handed out by Notsogood Ltd, and the value of those accounts, make it economically inadvisable to proceed with the setting up of an in-house collection agency. However, the high level and value of the accounts handed out by Worthwhile Ltd create a different picture. For this company there are genuine savings to be achieved and their in-house collection agency should be set up as follows.

☐ A direct telephone line needs to be installed for the sole use of the in-house agency. This phone should never be answered by the company's credit controllers. If the debtor recognises the voice of a credit controller the whole game plan will be blown.

☐ The credit controller(s) running the in-house agency should try to mentally divorce themselves from the company. An outside collection agency has only a very limited understanding of how its clients operate. If you display too much knowledge of the intricate workings of the company, the debtor may become suspicious.

☐ The in-house collection agency has to be set up with a separate trading address to avoid any connection being made with the company. Separate stationery needs to be printed for the sole use of the in-house collection agency. Post must be passed through a separate franking machine.

Solicitors

Choosing a solicitor to act for you in debt collection matters may not be as simple as you think. The legal firm your company uses for its other corporate affairs, will probably be the wrong one to use for your debt collection work. In the majority of cases, debt collection through the courts is not a complicated affair. However, it is time consuming; and, where solicitors are concerned, that means expensive.

If you hand accounts out to solicitors on a regular monthly basis, you would be best advised to use a firm that specialise in debt collection work. These firms will operate a computerised litigation system which can be dealt with quite adequately by a legal exec., thereby reducing your legal costs. Debt collection cases need to be handled by a fully fledged solicitor only if they progress to the seriously defended stage.

Solicitors' costs can vary quite substantially from firm to firm and, if you are intending to hand out a reasonable volume of work, you will be in a strong position to negotiate reduced rates. However, rates are not the only factor you need to look at. The ability to do the job quickly and efficiently is also of prime importance.

Many legal firms appear to be charging ridiculously low prices for their legal services. Don't be taken in by these costs, the firms are in business to make a profit just like the rest of us and they will need to make a profit from the accounts you pass to them as well. If a firm cannot be 'up-front' about the costs of their services, they are probably not worth dealing with. Remember, though: having chosen a firm of solicitors, it is costly to change them in the middle of a legal action. Take your time and choose right first time.

Using the courts for debt collection can be extremely expensive. If you become involved in seriously defended actions, your legal costs will increase sharply. At times like these it is worthwhile taking a close look at your solicitor's basic charges, such as the cost-per-letter that the solicitor sends. A few years ago, my company was involved in a complicated High Court case, where we eventually recovered £35,000. During this case, our solicitors sent out ninety six letters. By reducing their charge by £3 per letter, on this function alone we managed to achieve a £288 reduction in our legal costs.

As with your collection agency, you should monitor your legal cases on a regular basis to make sure action is continuing on them, and also monitor the individual costs of each case to see if it is cost-effective to continue with the action.

It is my personal belief that legal action should only be entered into, once all other options have failed. This is not because I feel a collection agency will be any more successful, but because I know they will be more cost-effective. In many cases, they will also generate the payment a little quicker.

8

COLLECTING DEBTS THROUGH THE COURTS

If you have been unsuccessful in collecting your debt through the normal collection process, you are faced with two options: either you can proceed with legal action to recover your debt, or you must accept it as bad and write it off.

Before you use the courts to recover your debt, you should at least try to ensure that legal action is a cost-effective alternative; once you have initiated legal action you are no longer totally in control of events, and as a result costs can escalate fairly rapidly.

When we embark on legal action, we all hope the debtor will pay on receipt of summons. However, this is not always the case; and so, before issuing legal proceedings, do make sure you have the resolve to see it through to the bitter end. Once you have entered into a legal action, it can be a costly affair to pull out before it has reached its conclusion.

Having decided to proceed with legal action, don't dither. You should proceed quickly in order to keep your debtor under pressure, and give yourself the best possible chance of success. The older a debt becomes, the more difficult it is to collect; and there is a greater risk of your debtor absconding, or not continuing to have the means to settle your debt.

Sometimes, credit controllers are wary of handing accounts out to solicitors, owing to the fact that they do not always have the best of reputations, especially when it comes to debt collection matters. It was

Samuel Johnson who said: "I do not wish to speak ill of any man behind his back, but I believe the gentleman is an attorney". Despite their reputation, solicitors can, and do, play a vital role in the collection of overdue debts.

Before proceeding with legal action you need to be fairly confident that your case is strong enough to win. It is pointless proceeding with an action that is unlikely to be successful, purely to satisfy a personal vendetta. Learning when to let go is an important part of credit management.

Having decided to proceed with legal action, your next step is to choose which court you want to issue in. As a general rule it will be cheaper to issue in the County Court. However, cost is not the only factor you need to look at when making a decision. You should also assess the length of time it will take to obtain judgement, and the most efficient way to enforce it.

The time delay that can occur in reaching the judgement stage is probably best emphasised by comparing the way each court deals with a defended action. In the High Court, if the defendant puts in a spurious defence, you can apply for a Summary Judgement to try to resolve the matter quickly. In the County Court, you cannot apply for Summary Judgement on debts under £3,000. All defended actions below this threshold, irrespective of whether the defence is valid or not, have to be referred to an Arbitration Hearing.

An Arbitration Hearing will usually be held in the defendant's home court, which means you may have to travel to the other end of the country to attend the hearing. Even if you are successful in winning the action, there is no guarantee that you will be awarded any of your costs or expenses associated with the hearing. In this scenario, using the County Court for recovery of debts below £3,000, to which there is no viable defence, would be more time consuming and expensive than using the High Court.

Each case you issue on is going to be different and should be considered on its own merits when deciding which court to use. In order to help you make this decision, I have detailed briefly the workings of each court, and hopefully this will give you a better understanding of the options available to you.

The County Court

The flow chart in *fig.8:1*, lists the procedure for collecting debts in the County Court, which has jurisdiction to deal with claims for trade debts of any value. However it does not have any jurisdiction in Scotland or Northern Ireland.

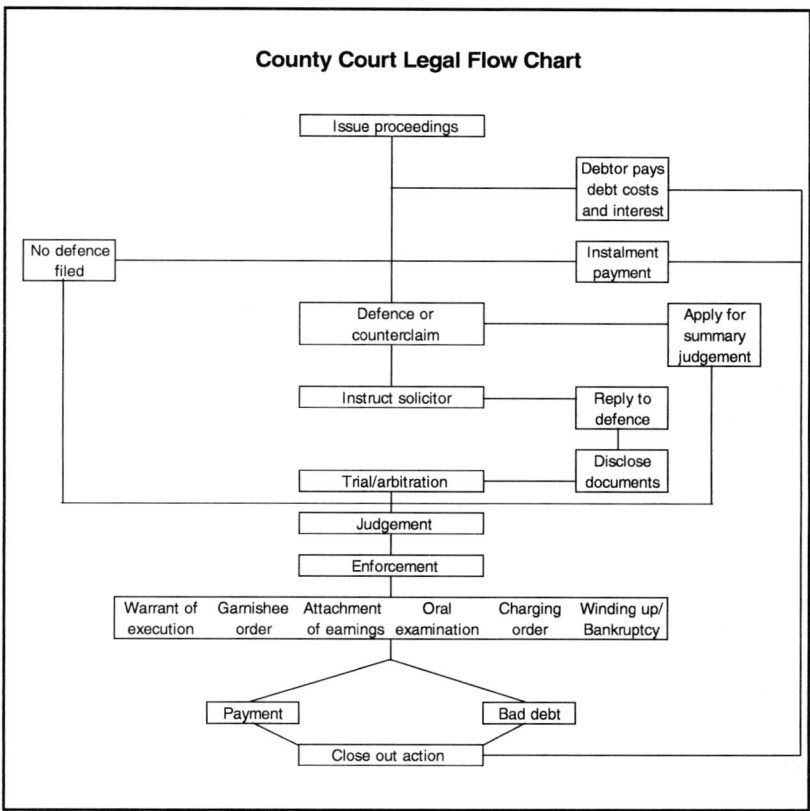

Fig. 8:1 Debt Collection Through The County Court.

The first step in the legal process is the issuing of a Default Summons, which the court serves on the defendant by post. If your debtor is the proprietor of a business you should sue him as an individual, trading as his business name. By issuing in this way you can enforce your judgement against the assets of the business or the individual. If your debtor is a partnership, you should sue each individual partner trading as their business name.

Where a limited company is concerned you need to issue in the registered name of the company, and ideally the summons should be served on the company's registered office, although you can serve at a trading address.

When issuing legal proceedings, it is imperative you issue in the correct name of the individual or company. If the name of your debtor company is Joe Bloggs (1981) Ltd, then you must issue as Joe Bloggs (1981) Ltd. Issuing in the name of Joe Bloggs Ltd is not sufficient, and could cause severe problems when you come to enforce your debt. Even if you have issued incorrectly, it is still possible that you will receive Judgement on your action; however, when you come to enforce the Judgement you will have problems, as you will be asking the Bailiff or Sheriff to seize the assets of a company or individual who does not exist. At this stage you will either have to apply for leave to amend the proceedings, or close out on your action and start all over again. Both options will be costly, and by the time you have resolved matters your debtor may have absconded, or become insolvent.

A summons is deemed as being issued once the court has authenticated it, and allocated a case number. The summons will then be posted to the defendant. The date the court posts the summons is classed as the date of service.

From the date of issue the defendant is liable for the original debt, costs, court fees and statutory interest. If the defendant pays your debt after the issue of the summons, but before he receives his copy through the post, he is still liable for the legal costs, court fees and statutory interest.

14 days after the service of the summons, and provided the defendant has not lodged a defence, you are entitled to enter judgement and instigate enforcement action. The various methods of enforcement will be discussed later in this chapter.

If the debtor enters a defence and/or counterclaim, you will have to proceed by one of three types of hearing. These hearings are now discussed in greater detail.

Arbitration Hearings

An Arbitration Hearing will normally be heard in the defendant's home court, and is held in the District Judge's chambers. This is a fairly informal hearing, where each party has the opportunity to put their case forward. The judge will then give his decision, which is binding on both parties.

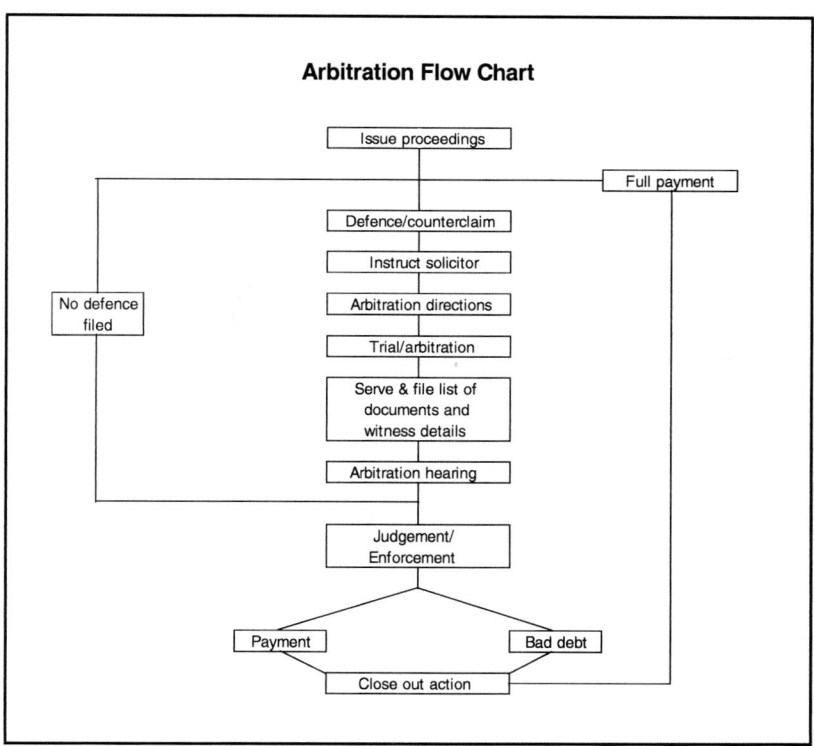

Fig. 8:2 Arbitration Flow Chart

An Arbitration Hearing will take place where the value of the plaintiff's claim does not exceed £3,000, and is the most common type of hearing carried out in the County Court. There is no official requirement for either party to be represented by a solicitor at these hearings. Unfortunately, at an Arbitration Hearing the plaintiff is unlikely to be reimbursed for any of his costs or expenses, even if he is successful in winning the action.

The flow chart in *fig.8:2* details the procedure for arbitration hearings in the County Court.

Summary judgement hearing

A plaintiff can only apply for Summary Judgement if the value of his debt is greater than £3,000. He would proceed in this manner if he felt the defence lodged by the defendant had no merit, and evidence could be produced to overturn it.

At the hearing, the District Judge will weigh up the affidavit evidence supplied by both sides, and decide whether the defendant has a valid defence. If the judge decides there is a triable issue, the case will proceed to a full trial in the defendant's home court. If on the other hand he throws out the defence, judgement will be entered in the plaintiff's favour, and the defendant will be ordered to pay the debt, costs, and interest. The defendant is usually given 14 days to comply with this order.

The advantages of applying for Summary Judgement are:

☐ If successful you can recover costs and expenses for this hearing.
☐ There is a long delay for full trial hearings in the County Court, therefore Summary Judgement will probably be the quickest way to achieve judgement on your debt.

The Full Trial

The Full Trial usually takes place in open court, and it is common for both parties to be represented by a solicitor or counsel. Unlike the Arbitration Hearing, the full trial is carried out on a more formal basis. As the hearing is in open court, the general public – and press – are entitled to attend.

Each side will have the option to call witnesses who will give evidence under oath, and face cross-examination by the opposing party or his legal representative. In order to reduce the length of time allotted to the full trial, each side is requested to exchange witnesses' statements before the actual trial begins. This may dispense with the need for a witness to give the bulk of his evidence orally in court, and once the party's legal representative has clarified a few points, the court can proceed swiftly to the cross-examination by the opposing side.

Having heard from both sides, the judge will consider the evidence that has been presented to him. He will already have seen the witness statements and documents lodged before the trial, and this will help to speed up his deliberation.

Having reached a decision, the judge will then give his summing up, where he will outline his thinking on the case, and then deliver his judgement. The judge will also make an order as to costs, which can be fairly high in a full trial.

There are two other hearings you may come across while taking debt recovery action in the County Court. The first is a Disposal Hearing, which occurs when the defendant offers to clear the debt by instalments, and the plaintiff refuses to accept the offer.

The disposal hearing will take place in the debtor's home court, and will be held in the District Judge's chambers. The judge will assess the defendant's offer, and his financial standing, and proceed to give his judgement. It is probably advisable to agree to any reasonable offer of instalment payments, as the judge nearly always comes down on the defendant's side in these matters, unless of course he is blatantly misrepresenting his financial standing. An order for disposal of fixed costs will usually accompany the judgement.

The other hearing is a Pre-Trial Review, or Directions Hearing which, as its name suggests, is carried out prior to the full trial. At this hearing, the District Judge reviews the situation in the case and makes an order as to what each party needs to do to get the action ready for trial. There is no need for either party to attend in person at a pre-trial review. It is simply a directions hearing which can be dealt with by the solicitors of each party.

The High Court

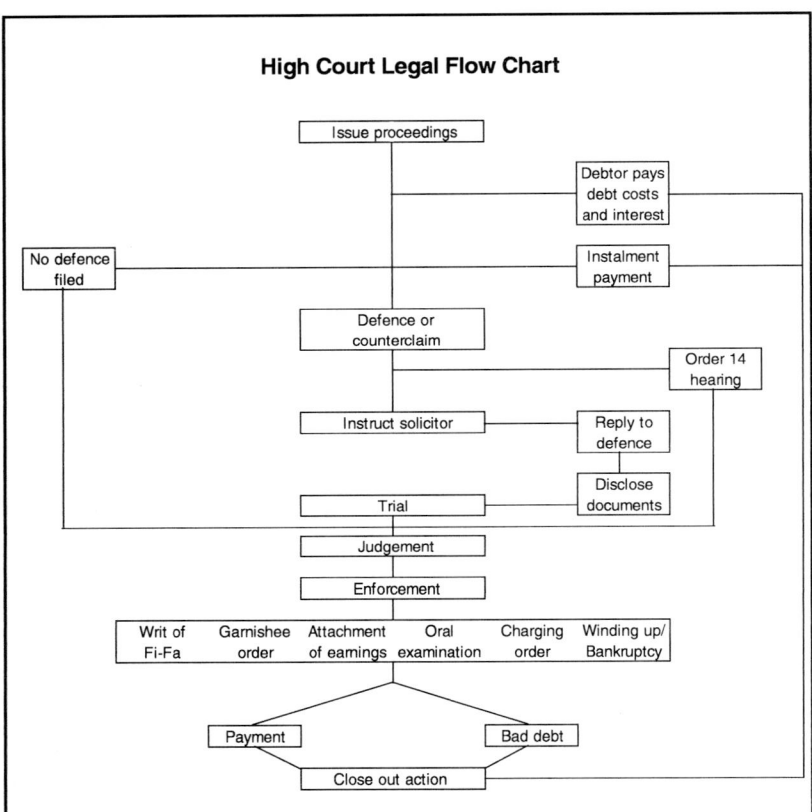

Fig. 8:3 Debt Collection Through The High Courts

As can be seen from the flow chart in *fig. 8:3*, the process for the recovery of debt through the High Court, is very similar to that of the County Court. However there are two important differences, and these are as follows:

Issuing proceedings

Proceedings are commenced in the High Court by way of issuing a writ against the defendant. The writ is sealed by the court, but unlike the County Court, the High Court does not serve proceedings. This is actioned by the plaintiff or his solicitors. The service can either be by post, or through personal service. However, service on a limited company is usually actioned by ordinary post to its registered office address.

Summary judgement

In the High Court there are no financial limits to bar the plaintiff from applying for summary judgement. Therefore, the process of obtaining judgement on debts below £3,000, where there is no valid defence to the action, is usually quicker through the High Court. However, on debts below £600 any award for costs is at the discretion of the Court.

Enforcement of a judgement debt

If you have received judgement in your favour, but the debtor has still refused to pay, the next step is to enforce the judgement. There are a number of ways you can achieve this; before I go on to discuss them I should state that you can transfer a judgement obtained in the County Court to the High Court and enforce it there, provided the debt is over £2,000.

On those occasions where I have to take action in the County Court, on receiving judgement I transfer matters to the High Court so that I can use the Sheriff's office to enforce the judgement. However, before you can transfer the judgement you need to obtain a certificate of judgement from the County Court. This will cause a slight delay between judgement and enforcement, but I consider this justifiable, as the service received from the Sheriff is often vastly superior to that received from the County Court bailiff.

Warrant of execution

A warrant of execution can be issued on judgements up to £5,000 in the County Court, and is enforced by the court bailiff. The bailiff will visit the defendant's premises in an effort to obtain payment. If he is unable to do so, he can take walking possession over the defendant's assets to cover your judgement debt plus removal and disposal costs.

The defendant is not allowed to dispose of these goods until such time as the warrant has been fully discharged, or a final return has been made by the bailiff. The debtor is usually given approximately seven days to pay your debt before his goods are removed for sale. However, if the bailiff is inundated with work, as they nearly always are, the time delay between walking possession and removal can be longer.

After the bailiff has taken walking possession it is not uncommon for him to receive a third party claim on some or all of the goods seized. This means that the goods are being claimed by a completely independent party, and are not owned by the defendant. If the assets do not belong to the defendant then they cannot be sold to clear his debt.

If you wish to challenge a third party claim, an Interpleader Summons will be issued, and a hearing will take place where the third party has to prove his title to the goods. Such matters can be costly and should be avoided if at all possible.

You should only proceed on an interpleader summons if you are sure you can overturn the third party claim. If you lose you will be liable for all costs and expenses associated with the hearing.

You will no doubt have heard a number of stories about the inefficiency of the County Court bailiff. Unfortunately most of them are true. The County Court bailiff service seems to be understaffed, and long delays can and will occur when you use this service. However it is not all bad news. There are proposals in the pipe line to privatise this service, which I believe can only result in an improved quality of service.

A writ of Fi-Fa

Not a song by Gilbert and Sullivan, a writ of Fi-Fa is the High Court equivalent to the Warrant of Execution; the difference being that the writ of Fi-Fa is executed by the Sheriff's Officer, as opposed to the bailiff.

The advantage of enforcing your judgement in the High Court is that the Sheriff is paid commission on the goods he recovers. The County Court bailiff is paid a flat wage whether he is successful or not. Which do you think is better motivated to recover the goods?

Garnishee order

If the defendant does not pay the judgement debt, but you believe he has the funds available to do so, an application can be made for a Garnishee Order.

A garnishee application is usually issued against the defendant's bank, effectively forcing it to freeze any money in the defendant's account, up to the amount of the judgement debt. The defendant is then informed of the situation, and given the time up to the hearing to clear the debt voluntarily. If the defendant fails to do so, his bank is ordered to pay the required amount into court.

When applying for a garnishee order, timing is of the essence, as you cannot garnishee against an overdrawn bank account. If you know your debtor is expecting a large cheque in two weeks' time, then delay your action to coincide with its arrival.

Before making an application for a garnishee order it may be worthwhile instructing an investigation company to obtain details of the balance of your debtor's bank account. You can then use this information to time your garnishee proceedings to perfection.

The information needed to instigate this action, such as the account name, account number and branch code, should be recorded on your credit application form – it may also be found on any recent cheques you may have received from your debtor.

Until recently, it was possible to obtain information on any bank account. However, the law has now changed and it is illegal to supply information on the bank accounts of private individuals.

Attachment of earnings

This method of enforcement is useful against a defendant who is in regular employment. In these cases, an attachment of earnings order is served on the defendant's employer, instructing them to deduct a given amount from the defendant's salary each month, which they have to pay into court. This continues until such time as your debt, costs and interest are recovered.

The problem with this type of enforcement is that it only works against individual debtors who are employed by a third party. It is not an option you can use against a limited company or a self-employed debtor, such as the proprietor of a business. These debtors have already ignored the court's instructions to pay the judgement debt, therefore it is very unlikely that they will abide by its order to deduct an amount from their own salary each month.

Oral examination

If the directors of a limited company are proving to be uncooperative in supplying you with relevant financial information on their company, it is possible to issue any or all of them, including the company secretary, with an order to appear at court for an oral examination.

The directors would then have to appear in court to answer specific questions and provide relevant financial information about the company. This information enables you to clarify the options open to you for the recovery of your debt, but you can still only proceed against the company and not the individual directors.

When applying to have a private individual orally examined, you should receive a detailed breakdown of their income and expenditure, which is useful when planning your enforcement strategy.

An oral examination is not a direct form of enforcement, and is therefore unlikely to lead directly to the payment of your debt, although there are the odd occasions where the debtor will pay the debt, rather than have to disclose private financial information to the court. The oral examination is basically used to obtain financial information that will help you in deciding whether it is economically viable to continue with your enforcement action.

Charging Order

The Charging Order is a long-term method of enforcement, and as such can only be effective if a property sale is coming up. A charging order can only be used against a debtor who owns his own property. At best it registers a charge against the debtor's property for the value of your judgement debt; but if the property is jointly owned, usually only a caution against dealings will be allowed.

You will often find that your charge is third in line. The building society with which the debtor is subject to a mortgage will normally have the first charge registered. The second charge will probably be registered by the debtor's bank to secure his overdraft or loan facilities. Another drawback with this type of enforcement action is that it is very long-term. You may not receive your money until the debtor sells his house, and only then provided there is enough equity in the property to clear the mortgage, together with any prior charges against the property.

A charging order can also be obtained on any shares held by the debtor. This form of enforcement really is a last desperate act to secure payment when all other forms of enforcement have failed, and where liquidation or bankruptcy are not financially sound options.

Liquidation and bankruptcy

Although it should not be considered directly as a method of enforcement, the threat of liquidation or bankruptcy is the ultimate action you can take to recover your debt. However, it may be pointless taking this action against an individual or a company that has no assets, or whose assets fall well short of its liabilities. This form of recovery is not cheap, therefore you need to be fairly certain that you are going to see some return on your debt.

When dealing with individuals, you are never sure exactly how much money they have. In these cases it may be advisable to issue a Statutory Demand to see if this leads to some form of payment proposal.

The only way in which a bankruptcy petition can be issued is upon non-compliance with a statutory demand, an unsatisfied writ of Fi-Fa, or warrant of execution.

The threat of bankruptcy proceedings tends to be more effective than the threat of winding up proceedings, and the reason for this is quite simple: the psychological pressure being placed on the individual is, in most cases, far greater than the pressure being placed on the directors of the limited company.

The directors of a limited company are not personally affected by the liquidation of their company unless it can be proved that they have been trading illegally or while knowing that the company was insolvent. Having had one company wound up they can, if they wish, set up a new company and continue trading as if nothing had happened. These debtors are often known as Phoenix companies

If an individual is made bankrupt, he and his family suffer directly from the action. His whole life may be affected for some years. Therefore the psychological impact of bankruptcy on an individual must be far greater. It is fair to assume that, the greater the psychological impact, the greater the chance the debtor will make some form of payment offer.

9

CREDIT CHECKING

The last decade has seen a considerable change in the way many companies credit check potential customers. The days of the bank and trade references are numbered, as tomorrow heralds a new dawn built upon the age of computer technology. Credit status reports, credit limits, and a detailed trading history of both company and director can be yours within minutes – all brought to you by the wonder of the on-line credit checking system.

Business information is one of the fastest areas of growth within the credit sector. Every year, new companies move into the market offering a greater variety of systems; and every year, this additional level of competition reduces the cost of on-line credit checking. There is no doubt that credit reporting has become big business, but is it really as important to the credit industry as its purveyors would have us believe?

The answer to this question is, without doubt, yes. Every bad debt that your company picks up will have started its life as an application for credit. Therefore, the more time and effort you put into credit checking your customers, the fewer bad debts your company is likely to incur during its normal trading activities.

By offering a new customer credit facilities, you are investing your company's resources in his business. This investment of credit is no different from a capital investment; you want to be sure you are going to see a return on your money, therefore thorough credit checks should be carried out in both cases.

Even with today's sophisticated technology, it is still practically impossible to eliminate bad debts; therefore, each individual business needs to calibrate its own credit sanctioning policy, allowing it to achieve results within its own control parameter.

The purpose of credit checking is to maintain an acceptable level of risk, not to eliminate trading altogether. If a company's credit sanctioning policy is too conservative, it will have the effect of stifling its sales activity. Without access to new customers and markets, a business cannot grow and prosper. Most companies in this situation would die a slow death through the natural erosion of their customer base.

The Credit Application Form

Any customer who applies for a credit account with your company should be asked to complete a credit application form. The format of these forms will vary from company to company, but the following information should always be requested as standard:

☐ The registered name of any limited company. The name of the partners if the company is a partnership. The name of the proprietor if the company is a sole trader.

☐ If the applicant is a limited company, you should obtain the address of its registered office, any trading addresses, its phone number and its registration number.

☐ If the applicant is a partnership or sole trader, the partners'/ proprietor's home addresses should be supplied, along with the trading address and phone number of the business.

☐ You should also record any other trading styles the applicant trades under.

☐ You should request details of two trade references.

☐ Bank details, along with a letter of authorisation, should also be requested so that you can contact the applicant's bank for a reference.

- ☐ Your application form should contain a clause that states: by applying for credit the customer agrees to be bound by your terms and conditions of sale – a copy of which should be printed on the back of your application form.
- ☐ The signature of the applicant with their name printed below in capitals, and their position in the company
- ☐ A monthly credit requirement

References and credit reports

Having received a completed credit application form, you now have three ways to check on the applicant's creditworthiness. These are:

- ☐ by taking up the trade references
- ☐ by taking up the bank references
- ☐ by obtaining a credit status report from a business information company.

Each of these options is now discussed in greater detail.

Trade references

From the experience I have gained over the last fifteen years, I have to say that in almost every case, the trade references supplied tend to be of little use. Only a fool would provide a potential supplier with references from customers with whom he had had a poor trading history; although I do remember one occasion where I received a reply that read:"Give him credit, you must be joking. I wouldn't lend him my bicycle." Needless to say, that applicant was not granted credit facilities.

One way to overcome the problem of obtaining a completely independent reference is to contact your competitors, claiming that your prospective customer has given their name as a trade reference. With luck you will find someone your applicant deals with, and obtain a totally unbiased opinion.

Apart from the question of honesty, there are two main problems associated with the use of trade references: first, the referee will not spend much time checking your applicant's trading history before completing the reference, so they are very rarely accurate. Secondly, the replies will take anything up to three weeks to be returned, if they come back at all. This causes seriously delays in your credit sanctioning process, and can lead to the loss of lucrative business.

Bank references

As with trade references, bank references can also be pretty inconclusive, especially for the uninitiated. However, once you have managed to master "bankspeak", they will be of some help; although I personally do not believe they should ever be used as a sole source of reference. The general rule of thumb suggests the shorter the reference, the more credit worthy the applicant is. I have listed below some of the more common replies that you will receive from a debtor's bank in answer to your request for a reference:

☐ "Undoubted" means the bank consider their client a very good trade risk for the figures you have quoted.
☐ "Good for your figure and purpose" means that their client is a reasonable trade risk, and that any commitments should be met.
☐ "Should prove good for your figures and purpose" means that you should go into more detail before you extend credit facilities.
☐ "Although their capital is fully employed we do not believe the directors would enter into a commitment they could not see their way to fulfil". Their client has cash flow problems, or is over-trading, and you should not touch them with a barge pole.

In March 1994, owing to outside pressure from independent review bodies, the major banks decided to amend their policy on issuing bank references. Although for many years these references had knowingly been passed on to people like you and me, they were originally intended as a way for banks to obtain information on customers for their own internal use. Today, all banks insist that bank reference requests are accompanied by a letter of authorisation from their customer, giving them permission to supply this information to a third party.

Business information publishers

One of the most effective ways to credit check limited companies is to subscribe to one of the leading business information publishers. Their on-line database systems are the quickest way to credit check a prospective customer; the speed associated with this form of credit checking is essential to companies that need to turn their credit applications around quickly. By using this type of service you can make a credit decision within five minutes, and that includes setting a credit limit.

Another area where on-line reports score over the old-fashioned trade and bank references is in their ability to supply you with detailed information relating to the company's trading history. Most reports will include the last three years' accounts, which enables you to analyse the direction in which the company is moving. Dun & Bradstreet reports also come with a payment score, which indicates how quickly your prospective customer pays his accounts. On occasion, however, this information can be misleading; and you should always check to see how many contributors have been used to calculate the score.

Business information companies can also be used to check for any County Court judgements or winding up petitions registered against your potential customer. Some also offer the opportunity of carrying out a directors' database search, which will enable you to review the trading history of a named director.

Unfortunately, these companies are not as successful when it comes to credit checking partnerships and sole traders. These types of businesses do not have to file accounts at Companies House, therefore it is difficult to obtain financial information on them. Although business information publishers are making efforts to improve their hit rate, in most cases you will have to revert back to your bank and trade references.

Status reports can be expensive, especially if your company has a transient customer base and therefore carries out a large number of credit checks each month. These reports do vary in price depending on which company you use, the amount of information required, and the number of enquires made during the year; and substantial discounts are always on offer for bulk usage.

Don't be fooled into thinking that all business information publishers offer the same information. The main thrust of their information may be the same, however the sundry information or options they offer can make all the difference. You also need to take into account the quality and accuracy of the information supplied, and how user-friendly the on-line software package is. You need a quick and reliable service, of course – but this may not always be the cheapest option.

I use Experian (formerly CCN) for all my business information needs, however this is a personal choice, and you need to use the system that best suits your company's situation.

Trade groups

Another way for you to obtain an independent reference is to join an industry trade group, where you share credit information during regular monthly meetings. These trade groups are growing in popularity, and are a useful and cost-effective way of obtaining credit information. However, you must make sure that you do not work too closely as a group. This can lead to accusations that you are restricting trade, and therefore operating illegally as a cartel.

Ratio analysis

There will always be a special place in my affections for the art of ratio analysis. I find it fascinating to look at a company's past trading performance, calculate its current position, and use the trends that appear from this analysis to predict the company's future trading prospects. I could no more fly in the air, than write a book on credit management that did not cover this topic.

Unfortunately, I have to admit that, with the growth and quality of the information supplied by companies such as Experian, the need for a credit manager to be able to analyse a set of accounts is slowly declining. However, status reports from business information companies can be expensive and are not always geared to suit your company's individual needs. With this in mind, I feel that all credit controllers should be able to carry out a basic form of analysis, if only to show them why companies fail, and how to spot the warning signs that usually precede a failure.

A company's ability to meet its future liabilities is directly linked to its historic trading performance. Because of this, you cannot successfully analyse a company's trading performance purely from its latest balance sheet. This is nothing more than a photograph of a company's trading activity, taken at a particular hour, on a particular day. In two months' time the picture could be totally different.

When measuring a company's trading performance, you should always look at the last three years' accounts, and if possible the last five. This allows you to calculate relevant ratios for a substantial period, and will highlight any trends showing whether the company's trading position is improving or declining.

When you analyse a company's accounts, the two areas of most importance to you are liquidity and profitability. The analysis for each of these is now discussed in greater detail. All ratio calculations will be taken from the tables in *figs. 9:1* and *9:2*, which list extracts from the last five years' accounts for Feeling Fine Ltd, and On The Slide Ltd.

Liquidity

A company's liquidity ratio is probably the most important area of analysis for potential lenders. Analysis of this section of a company's accounts will indicate how liquid the company is, and therefore how quickly it can pay your account. The first liquidity ratio we are going to look at is the current ratio (current assets/current liabilities). Current assets are assets that can be turned into cash within one year, i.e., stock, debtors, cash. Current liabilities are liabilities that need to be met within one year, i.e., creditors, bank overdraft, short-term loan, and other accrued charges.

Feeling Fine Ltd

	1991	1992	1993	1994	1995
Sales	500,000	600,000	700,000	800,000	900,000
Purchases	300,000	400,000	500,000	600,000	700,000
Current assets	440,000	520,000	600,000	680,000	760,000
Current liabilities	360,000	410,000	470,000	520,000	560,000
Working capital	80,000	110,000	130,000	160,000	200,000
Stock	200,000	210,000	215,000	220,000	225,000
Debtors	190,000	230,000	260,000	290,000	310,000
Creditors	320,000	365,000	420,000	460,000	480,000
Gross profit	45,000	57,000	70,000	84,000	99,000
Net profit before tax	20,000	27,000	35,000	44,000	54,000
Retained earnings	200,000	216,200	237,200	263,600	296,000

Fig. 9:1 Trading Performance for Feeling Fine Ltd

On the Slide Ltd

	1991	1992	1993	1994	1995
Sales	500,000	600,000	700,000	800,000	900,000
Purchases	300,000	400,000	500,000	600,000	700,000
Current assets	390,000	440,000	500,000	550,000	590,000
Current liabilities	410,000	500,000	600,000	670,000	725,000
Working capital	-20,000	-60,000	-100,000	-120,000	-135,000
Stock	190,000	210,000	230,000	260,000	285,000
Debtors	130,000	170,000	200,000	230,000	270,000
Creditors	240,000	255,000	290,000	320,000	356,000
Gross profit	25,000	20,000	16,000	13,000	5,000
Net profit before tax	11,000	8,000	4,000	1,000	-4,000
Retained earnings	30,000	34,800	37,200	37,800	33,800

Fig. 9:2 Trading performance for On The Slide Ltd

In 1995, Feeling Fine Ltd had current assets of £760,000 and current liabilities of £560,000. This equates to a current ratio of 1.36:1, (760,000/560,000). Any business showing a current ratio in excess of 1:1 should not have any problems paying your account on time. In fact, with adequate cash management controls, companies can survive quite happily with current ratios as low as .80:1. However, extreme caution should be used if a company falls below this level.

If we now take a look at On The Slide Ltd (*fig. 9:2*), we can see that it has current assets of £560,000, while its current liabilities total £760,000. This equates to a current ratio of 0.81:1, (560,000/760,000). Although this figure is nowhere near as good as that of Feeling Fine Ltd, it is just above the point where we should be seriously concerned.

Over the years, analysts have discovered that the current ratio can be a little misleading. This is especially true if the company is carrying high levels of stock, or when the ratio calculation falls into that grey area around .80:1.

The acid test, also known as the 'quick ratio', deducts stock from the current assets before measuring them against the current liabilities (current assets less stock/current liabilities). The reason for this is that it would be difficult to convert all your stock into cash within a short period of time. In fact the only way to achieve this would probably be to cease trading and sell the stock at a large discount. When carrying out this analysis you should still be looking for a ratio of 1:1 or greater. However, as with the current ratio, there is still a grey area between 0.8:1 and 1:1, where companies can survive providing they are exercising control over their cash flow.

If we look at the acid test ratio for Feeling Fine Ltd, as calculated from its 1995 trading results, we see that it equates to 0.96:1, (£760,000 – £225,000 ÷ £560,000). This is at the upper end of your control band, and should not cause the company any problems. Unfortunately the same cannot be said for On The Slide Ltd, whose acid test ratio for the trading year of 1995 equates to 0.42:1, (£590,000 – £285,000 ÷ 725,000). This is well outside your control band, and should cause concern to anyone offering credit facilities.

The acid test result for On The Slide Ltd, shows how distorting the current ratio can be. In the first example, On The Slide Ltd had a current ratio of 0.8:1, just inside your control band. The acid test indicates how much of its current assets were made up of stock, and therefore could not readily be converted into cash. When looking at the acid test ratio, it becomes apparent that On The Slide Ltd is suffering severe cash flow problems, and as such may be a poor credit risk.

We now need to take the credit analysis a step further. It could be that 1995 was a poor year for On The Slide Ltd, and totally out of character with its previous trading performances. In order to clarify this we need to look at more than one year's trading results. As stated earlier in this chapter, one year's trading results will not give you a clear picture of a company's trading position. What is important is the trend that develops when you compare results over a number of years.

If a company's liquidity is increasing year on year, it is fair to assume that the company will still be trading next year. If the trend shows a continuous decline in the company's liquidity then the same can not be said. If the company's liquidity performance fluctuates regularly over the five year period, then it is fair to assume the company will survive, however greater caution should be given to the setting of credit limits.

Fig. 9:3 shows the liquidity trend for Feeling Fine Ltd, and On The Slide Ltd. Which company do you feel is most likely to be around next year?

Current Ratio					
	1991	1992	1993	1994	1995
Feeling Fine Ltd	1.22:1	1.27:1	1.28:1	1.31:1	1.36:1
On the Slide Ltd	0.92:1	0.88:1	0.83:1	0.82:1	0.81:1
Acid Test					
	1991	1992	1993	1994	1995
Feeling Fine Ltd	0.66:1	0.76:1	0.82:1	0.88:1	0.96:1
On the Slide Ltd	0.49:1	0.46:1	0.45:1	0.43:1	0.42:1

Fig. 9:3 Liquidity ratio trends for Feeling Fine Ltd & On The Slide Ltd

Profitability

Just because a company is profitable it does not necessarily mean that it is going to continue to trade. Although profitability plays an important part in a company's survival, more businesses fail because they have poor cash flow, than for any other reason. However, if a company has been trading at a loss and shows little sign of returning to profit in the near future, it is unlikely that its directors, or its bankers, will continue to finance its trading. For this reason, profitability ratios are a very important indication of the level of risk you will be taking, should you offer credit facilities.

The two ratios I use most frequently to measure profitability are as follows.

☐ Gross profit/sales (%)
☐ Net profit before tax/sales (%) (also known as the profit margin)

Gross Profit					
	1991	1992	1993	1994	1995
Feeling Fine Ltd	9.0%	9.5%	10.0%	10.5%	11.0%
On the Slide Ltd	5.0%	3.3%	2.3%	1.6%	0.5%
Profit Margin					
	1991	1992	1993	1994	1995
Feeling Fine Ltd	4.0%	4.5%	5.0%	5.5%	6.0%
On the Slide Ltd	2.2%	1.3%	0.6%	0.1%	-0.4%

Fig. 9:4 Profit ratios

As can be seen from *fig. 9:4,* Feeling Fine Ltd has increased both its gross profit and profit margin year on year over the last five years. This is a strong indication that the company is being well run, and that its trading costs are well under control. If these results are taken in conjunction with its liquidity ratio, Feeling Fine's prospects for future development seem excellent. You should not have any hesitation in extending credit facilities to this company.

Unfortunately the future does not look so good for On The Slide Ltd. Its profitability has fallen consecutively for the last five years. This has culminated in the company making a trading loss of £4,000 in 1995. The company has traded profitably in the past, as can be seen from its retained earnings figure shown in *fig. 9:2*. However given its present loss-making position, and its serious liquidity problems, it is unlikely On The Slide Ltd will make it through the year. With this in mind, all purchases made from your company should be on a pro-forma basis.

Other ratios that it is useful to calculate when analysing a company's creditworthiness are:

- ☐ Days sales outstanding (debtors x 365/sales)
- ☐ Creditors ratio (creditors x 365/purchases)

The days sales outstanding (DSO) figure highlights how quickly the company is collecting its debt. A poor rate of collection can lead to cash flow problems, and thence delays in the payment of your account. The creditors ratio shows how quickly the company pays its debts, and so highlights how quickly you are likely to get paid. If these two ratios are out of , it is likely to place pressure on the company's cash flow. Therefore you would ideally like to see these two ratios in a state of equilibrium.

Credit checking can be carried out on many levels, including the building of computerised models of the economy, through which you can gauge how certain events may affect the trading position of your prospective customer. However, for normal day-to-day decisions, most credit controllers will not need to go beyond the level of credit checking laid down in this chapter.

10

STRESS MANAGEMENT

Stress is probably the most written about aspect of management today. It is essential for a manager to have an understanding of the causes of stress in the workplace if he is to obtain maximum efficiency from his workforce. In the next few pages I will try to give you a layman's view of what stress is, how everyday working routines can trigger stress, and suggest ways to overcome these stressors.

The most important thing to remember is that we are all individuals and as such will react to, and cope with, the pressures of life in different ways. A person's disposition will usually determine the level of their stress reaction. Some people seem to be addicted to the buzz they receive from being under pressure. This type of person tends to cope well with high levels of stress. Others by their very nature are born worriers. These individuals prefer to expose themselves to much lower levels of stress. While you can adapt your lifestyle to meet your desired stress level, you cannot avoid it altogether; the stimuli that cause stress surround you in your everyday life.

Contrary to popular belief, the stimuli that cause stress do not have to be negative; positive stimuli may be just as potent. Can you remember those halcyon days of your first love? Do you remember the first time you spoke to her, how your mouth was so dry it was hard to speak clearly; your stomach was churning away, and your head was swimming with the smell of her perfume? Remember how your hands were shaking uncontrollably, and your heart was pounding so hard that you thought it would burst through your chest? Well, I am sorry to spoil your illusions but you were not experiencing love; love is something totally different. All the symptoms listed above are in fact the body's natural response to stress. Whether the stimuli are positive or negative the response is the same.

What is stress?

For many years the theory of stress was a hotly disputed subject. However, in recent years the medical profession seems to be uniting behind Professor Hans Selye's theory of the General Adaption System. This theory concentrates on the response of the body and brain to stress stimuli. Selye discovered that the the pattern of stress follows three stages: first is the alarm reaction, which is the system's initial response to the stressors. This is also known as the 'fight or flight' reaction. During this stage, adrenalin is discharged into the body causing physiological changes. At the same time, large quantities of sugar and cholesterol are released into the bloodstream to meet the expected increase in energy requirements.

The pupils of the eyes dilate and your hearing becomes more acute. This enables you to hear and see better. You start to breathe faster, and your heartbeat increases, supplying more oxygen (the body's fuel), to the muscles and brain. This enables you to think and to run faster. It also increases your body strength if you intend to stand and fight.

In normal circumstances, once the emergency has been dealt with, the body will return to a state of equilibrium. However, in the individual who is under constant stress the body hardly ever returns to normal. If this situation is sustained over a period of time, the sufferer moves to the second level of stress.

The second stage is that of resistance, when mind and body attempt to deal with the problems caused by the stressors but are denied the natural release of 'fight or flight'. Having been unable to recover from the first stage of stress and return to a state of equilibrium, the body responds by asking for more energy to combat the stress. This request for extra energy is met by the release of more powerful chemicals into the bloodstream, known as cortico-steroids. At the same time, the body also releases extra levels of fat and sugar to fuel the new energy demand. However, if the stress reactions still cannot be controlled, the body will deem the energy level to be inadequate. The cortico-steroids then proceed to shut down the immune system to help save energy. This then leaves you open to the threat of infection, and is one reason why long-term suffers of stress always seem to be suffering from one ailment after another.

The third stage of stress is inevitably that of exhaustion. By this point your resistance has proven inadequate, and mental breakdown or severe psychical illness is likely to occur.

The problem society has today is that the stimuli which trigger stress have evolved, while our physical reaction to stress has not. Most of the stimuli you face in the workplace cannot be dealt with by the flight or fight reaction. This reaction is designed to help you in life-threatening situations, it is of little practical use to you when you are receiving a dressing-down from the Financial Director. With this in mind you need to develop your lifestyle to enable you to control stress in its initial stage, before it reaches the more harmful resistance stage.

Stress In the Workplace

Recent surveys have shown that stress now accounts for the loss of more working days annually than industrial action. It has been calculated that the British economy loses £3.2 billion a year through stress-related absenteeism.

People are usually the most costly element of any organisation's budget, especially when they start to malfunction; so why is it that companies tend to be more concerned with maintaining machinery than they are with maintaining the health of their employees? Much of the stress found in the workplace could be avoided if only employers would take the time to communicate with their managers.

The latest research carried out by the Health & Safety Executive, has shown that stress within corporate structures tends to follow the company's own pyramid formation, with manual workers suffering the most and top executives the least. There are two main reasons why corporate stress takes this form. First, workers who have little control over their day-to-day activities are more prone to stress. Secondly, people who carry out a task with a high degree of responsibility, but a low degree of authority (the perfect description of a credit controller?), are more likely to suffer from stress.

The causes of stress in the workplace can be broken down into two categories: aspects of work, and aspects of the environment. Let us now take a closer look at these.

Aspects of work

The main contributors to stress within this category are:

Lack of control or involvement in decisions.

We all hate having decisions made for us. We like to feel we have some control over our lives, even in our work environment. Decisions that are imposed on a workforce without discussion, even if they are the right decisions, will be met with resistance. Psychologists have shown that a workforce will make more of an effort to achieve a goal that they had some input in, than one that is imposed on them.

How often have you found that changes to working practices are imposed on a credit control department without any form of consultation? To make matters worse, these changes are usually devised by senior managers who have little understanding of the requirements necessary to run a successful credit control function. As a result, these changes are usually unworkable – six months down the line they have to be rescinded.

This type of problem is probably one of the greatest causes of stress within the workplace, yet is so easily avoided. If the credit manager was consulted before the changes were implemented, the problem would not arise. He is the best-placed person to know how to achieve the desired results; as such, he will be able to discuss the new requirements with the credit controllers and involve them in any decisions made.

Obviously, a department cannot be run on a policy of total consensus. In the end the right decisions have to be made, and goals have to be achieved. The secret is to encourage your staff to come up with the right method to achieve the goals set.

Repetitive and Dull Tasks

In my experience, good credit controllers make terrible administrators. They love the cut and thrust of the chase, but hate the mundane clerical side of the job. Credit controllers see tasks such as faxing copy invoices, filling invoices and writing out collection agency forms and journals as mundane tasks that keep them away from where the real action is. Good credit controllers are driven by one desire, and one desire only: to collect money owed to the company. Before you start to worry, let me put your mind at rest; what I am talking about here is their work-related desires. One imagines, hopes even, that their personal desires are somewhat different.

We all have to carry out some mundane tasks during the course of the working day, and credit controllers are no different in this respect. The real problem arises when the level of admin increases disproportionately, and results in too much time being spent on mundane tasks, and too little on the primary function. When this happens, staff become demotivated and stress can be triggered.

A short while ago, the company I work for installed a new computerised chase system. The system itself is excellent and provides a lot of useful trading information on the customers we deal with. The problem with computers is that the more information they are programmed to give you, the more data you need to feed them in the first place. A few months after its installation, it became clear to me that all was not as it should be: we were falling short of our forecast call levels, and as a result less money was being collected.

After discussing the problem with the credit controllers, I carried out an analysis of how they were spending their working day. To my horror, I found that, since swapping to our new system, the credit controllers were spending over half their working day on admin tasks.

However, this was only part of the problem: the credit controllers knew that they could not generate enough time during the day to make the calls necessary to hit their cash collection targets. This led to a feeling of frustration, and increased levels of stress, which slowed down the working process even further.

I believe that this cause of stress can be eradicated totally, by employing credit control clerks to deal with the admin side of the department. This would allow credit controllers to concentrate on their primary function, and would probably lead to admin duties being carried out more efficiently and cost-effectively than they would if they remained in the hands of the credit controllers.

Lack of managerial support

It is not uncommon for credit managers to suffer from a lack of managerial support in the day-to-day running of their departments. Without the support of their line manager, they will find it difficult to carry out their job to the best of their ability. If this occurs over a sustained period they will become demotivated; this will lead to increased levels of stress, and affect the way they manage their departments.

A lack of support for credit managers usually stems from a line manager's ignorance of the requirements needed to run a successful credit control function. If as a credit manager you suffer from this problem, your only hope is to educate your superior in the needs and importance of the credit control process. In most cases, if the superior is approached in the right way, the situation can be resolved.

Aspects of the working environment

The environment in which we work plays a very important part in the way we perform, as the study of ergonomics has demonstrated that changing a company's working environment for the better will reduce stress levels and improve output. Areas of the working environment highlighted by the Health & Safety executive as most likely to cause stress are as follows:

Space

Overcrowding is one of the most common stressors to be found in the workplace today. We all need our individual space and subconsciously operate our own personal exclusion zone – our own space which we do not like anyone else entering, other than at our personal request. An overpopulated office encroaches on this space, causing tension and stress.

Noise

Noise is another cause of stress in the workplace. Today's high-tech office tends to have a constant drone of computers, printers, photocopiers,and facsimile machines acting as a noisy backdrop to the normal, everyday office activities. This tends to break concentration and leads to reduced levels of output and performance.

Fortunately all is not lost. Some forward-looking organisations are beginning to wake up to the advantages improved working conditions can have on staff performance. The remainder are slowly being coerced into improving conditions through the implementation of EU legislation.

When looking at these aspects of your working environment it is tempting to consider each problem in isolation, marginalizing its importance. What organisations need to remember is that it is very rare for problems to come in ones: for example, an overmanned office is likely also to be overpopulated with machinery. This means that it will almost certainly be a noisy office in which to work, increasing the pressures of proximity to other stressed-out employees. Unfortunately the problems do not stop here, as frantic employees and their office equipment will both contribute to a rise in the ambient temperature, making the office unbearably stuffy during the Summer months.

The office detailed above is already falling foul of three of the negative environmental problems that can lead to stress: noise, overpopulation and temperature. Research carried out by the Health & Safety Executive has shown that these problems are high on the list of negative stimuli that will lead to stress among the workforce. Most workplaces also suffer from at least one of the following ills: poor access to natural light, badly designed office furniture and open-plan areas, giving no privacy or 'personal space'.

As you start to add these separate aspects together it becomes very clear how important our working environment is, and how it can effect both our health and the company's profitability.

The effect of stress on output

Credit control is by its very nature a stressful occupation. Therefore it is most important that everything possible is done to keep outside stressors to a minimum. If the level of stress within the credit control department is allowed to rise unchecked, companies will soon find that their collection performance suffers.

Apart from the immense personal costs of stress-related symptoms such as alcoholism, coronary heart disease and divorce, the commercial costs of stress are high for worker and employer alike; the most common ones being: increased absenteeism, job dissatisfaction, poor levels of worker co.-operation, operational mistakes and high levels of staff turnover. These inexorably result in higher employment costs, less money being collected, and the likelihood of increased levels of bad debts.

At the end of the day, stress in the workplace is a corporate problem that needs to be resolved at the highest level. However this does not excuse the credit manager from spotting the symptoms of stress in his workforce at an early stage, and doing everything in his power to dissipate it. I have listed below some of the more common symptoms to watch out for.

The symptoms of stress

Behavioural symptoms

☐ overreacting to situations, with laughter or irritability.
☐ uncommunicative behaviour

- □ inability to switch off problems
- □ difficulty in making decisions
- □ inability to react quickly to problems
- □ increased absenteeism
- □ relying on rules rather than using creative thinking.
- □ increasing lateness
- □ leaving for home a few minutes early
- □ clock watching
- □ long lunch breaks
- □ excessive trips to the toilet

Physical symptoms

- □ excessive sweating
- □ trembling
- □ inarticulate or stuttering speech
- □ change in eye contact
- □ frequent colds
- □ nervous tics
- □ rapid weight gain or loss.

Of course, some of these symptoms may be evidence of more serious problems such as drug-taking, alcoholism or illness, and the advice of the company doctor should be sought in extreme cases, or where a friendly word with the individual concerned does not reveal the true nature of the problem.

As stated earlier in this chapter there is no such thing as a stress-free zone. There will always be stress within the workplace, as there will be in every other aspect of your life. Stress is not all bad. Positive stress can be productive; it hones your body to its peak condition, allowing you to perform consistently within the top range of your capabilities. However, organisations should not use this as an excuse to ignore the debilitating effects of negative stress.

Enormous strides could be made in the reduction of stress, if only organisations would allow their employees some form of input into the everyday working decisions that affect their lives. The break-through will only come when companies accept that stress is not in itself an illness, but a normal physiological reaction that can be controlled and turned to their benefit through the right form of managerial support. I have listed below a few procedures which, if implemented, might reduce stress levels within your own working environment:

☐ Make sure you are suited to credit control. It is a stressful profession at the best of times, and if you find it difficult to communicate effectively on the phone, or assert yourself in a controlled way, it will be an impossible job for you to do.

☐ Try to organise regular monthly meetings with managers of other departments who have an input into the credit control process. This will enable you to discuss any malfunctions occurring in their departments, and resolve them at an early stage, thereby averting any serious breakdown in systems.

☐ Try to use your influence to develop your company's accounting system to give the maximum level of support to you and your department. Obviously a certain amount of negotiation is necessary, as there will always be differing points of view. However if you proceed in the right way you should be able to gain most of your requirements.

☐ Keep the office as tidy as possible. A cluttered office gives the impression of a lack of space and threatening disorder.

☐ Keep background noise to a realistic minimum. People do find it hard to concentrate within a noisy environment.

☐ Have regular monthly meetings with all credit control staff allowing them an input into the way the department is run (within reason).

☐ Make sure your staff are aware that the company appreciates their efforts, especially in times of great stress such as when installing a new computer system. During this period results may not be at their best, and your team need to know that you understand the reasons for this.

☐ Carry out regular motivation tests on your staff to make sure their individual motives are being stimulated. A motivated person is unlikely to suffer high levels of stress.

☐ Make sure your department is made aware of the success it is achieving. People who are successful at what they do are unlikely to suffer high levels of stress.

☐ Try not to overpopulate the office. Cramped office conditions lead to a high level of background noise and the invasion of your personal space. Both these conditions can lead to stress.

☐ Eating healthily and working out regularly will help to burn up the excess sugar and cholesterol caused by stress, thereby creating a more healthy lifestyle.

☐ If you can convince your company to pay for them, stress management courses are well worth looking at. Gentle exercise and controlled breathing techniques can help you remain in control in a stressful situation. I am also a great believer in aromatherapy and reflexology to help reduce the symptoms of stress.

At some time in the future, evolution will correct the imbalance that has occurred between modern-day stressors, and our reaction to them. Unfortunately, evolution measures time in generations, not years. Therefore the resolution of this problem, as far as ourselves and our children are concerned, rests firmly in our hands. For all our sakes I hope we learn to recognise the destructive nature of stress, and how to adapt our work patterns to cope with it, before it is too late.

11

WHY DO WE NEED CREDIT CONTROL?

Why do we need credit control? How often have you heard someone say: "But he always pays his account eventually, what does it matter if it is not today?" The reason it matters is quite simple: businesses need cash flow to survive, in the same way as you or I do.

Maybe the easiest way to explain this is to imagine what would happen if your employer came to you one day and said that he intended to pay you your salary, of course, but there would be a delay of one month. Presumably you are like me and do not have a small fortune tucked away under your bed, so what problems would this cause you? Are all the people you owe money to going to wait an extra month to be paid? Will the supermarket let you walk away with your monthly shopping on the promise of payment next month? You have to agree, it is not very likely. So you are now faced with the need to generate cash quickly to meet your monthly commitments. The obvious way to achieve this is to go into debt. You arrange an over-draft facility with your bank, and – provided your wages are usually paid into your account each month – this should not be a problem.

Assuming your employer keeps his word and pays you two months salary the following month, you will be back to square one. Well, actually, not quite square one. Like any company that fails to collect its debts on time, you will have to suffer the interest charges on your overdraft facility; therefore the amount of salary you have received has been effectively reduced.

Let us now take this scenario one step further: what happens if, at the end of the second month, your employer still has problems and will not be able to pay you until the end of the *following* month? Unless you are extremely lucky and win on the lottery, and we all know what are the odds against that, you have little option other than to go back to your bank. Only this time they may not be so accommodating. They may feel that their money is at risk. If they do they will increase their overdraft charges to reflect the greater risk. They will also deduct last month's interest charges from any money advanced to you. This will result in a reduction in the amount of money available for you to spend, which will affect your standard of living, and may very well lead to you being unable to meet all your commitments (you are suffering from cash flow problems, remember).

If the same thing happens the following month, the bank will almost certainly look for security on its loan. This would probably take the form of a charging order against your property, or any other assets of value you may have. Before long, you find that most of your money is being used up on interest charges and you can no longer afford to live. At this stage the bank will not lend you any more money, and will call in their loan – forcing you into bankruptcy. (Although your employer has every intention of paying you the money he owes you, the delay in receiving this money has led to you becoming insolvent).

I appreciate that, unless we are dealing with a very small business, one customer paying late will not seriously affect a company's cash flow; the problem is, it never is just one customer. Somehow, other customers find out, and before long everyone is after extended credit. The bank may allow a business longer to resolve its cash flow problem, but at the end of the day the company will suffer the same fate as you or I. This is why it is important that customers pay their account today. Not tomorrow, not next week, or next month, but today.

You will undoubtedly find that most of your company's debtors have every intention of paying their account as soon as funds become available. Unfortunately, good intentions do not put money in the bank, or finance a company's trading activities.

At this stage I should point out that some companies will have the resources to be able to trade quite happily, even though they may be taking 90 days or more to collect their debts. Although these companies will not be experiencing cash flow problems, they will not be maximising their profit levels either; and as a result their growth potential will suffer.

Having explained why an effective credit control function is necessary to create cash flow, let us take a more detailed look at the importance of cash flow, and the devastating effect that failing to control it can have on a company's trading profit.

The importance of cash flow

During the recession of the 'nineties, 'cash flow' became something of a buzz-word. It seemed that every customer you spoke to had a cash flow problem, and needed extra time to pay his account. What these customers were actually experiencing was a problem with short-term cash flow, the money a company needs on a day-to-day basis in order to survive. However: sustained, long-term cash flow is also vitally necessary if a company is to develop and grow.

The growth of any business is to a great extent dictated by the level of cash available to it. If, due to an ineffective credit control function, companies are forced to use their overdraft or loan capital to finance their sales ledger, they will find it impossible to achieve the growth necessary to survive. This inability to generate long-term cash flow usually affects small businesses, especially during a protracted recession.

If businesses cannot develop long-term cash flow they stagnate and eventually die. In the UK, the average life expectancy of a business is only ten years. If we are to increase this average, and offer the workforce greater job security, businesses need to achieve two things: first, they need to control their costs; and secondly, they need to control their debtor base.

On average in the UK it takes a business 78 days to collect payment for the credit it extends. This level of days sales outstanding (DSO) allows a business to turn over its cash (money owed by its debtors) only 4.68 times in the course of a year. If a company managed to collect all its debts on 30 days, however, it could increase this figure to 12.17 cash turns per annum. The higher the number of cash turns a company can generate in the course of a year, the lower its DSO level becomes, and the greater the increase in the company's cash flow. This increased cash flow can be used to meet the company's cash requirements; and as a result, loan capital or retained profit can be used to finance the company's expansion needs.

The table in *fig. 11:1*, shows the relationship between a company's DSO and its cash flow, and highlights how its cash flow can be increased through better control of its debtor base.

DSO	Cash turns	Increase in cash flows compared to UK average
78	4.68	UK average
75	4.87	4.1%
70	5.21	11.3%
65	5.62	20.1%
60	6.08	29.9%
55	6.64	41.9%
50	7.30	56.0%
45	8.11	73.3%
40	9.13	95.1%
35	10.43	122.9%
30	12.17	160.0%

Fig. 11:1 The relationship between a company's DSO and its cash flow

Increasing the number of cash turns generated in the course of a year will help to increase a company's profit level, as can be seen from the following example:

Quickcash Ltd has credit sales of £20,000,000 and finances its debtor base through an overdraft facility at an interest charge of 15 per cent per annum.

Assuming Quickcash has a DSO of 78 days (4.68 cash turns), the cost of financing its £20,000,000 of credit sales will be £641,096 (£20,000,000 x 15%/365 x 78). However, if Quickcash implements a tougher credit control policy, which results in a reduction in its DSO level to 58 days, its finance costs will reduce to £476,712 (£20,000,000 x 15%/365 x 58) This results in a reduced finance charge, and increased profits of £164,384 per annum.

Without increasing its level of sales one iota, Quickcash Ltd has been able to increase its profits by £164,384. It is worth remembering this when senior management try to tell you that credit control as a function does not generate revenue.

The effects of poor credit control

The way companies carry out their credit control function has a wider impact than they may at first imagine. A prime example of this can be found with small businesses, who during the recession accepted long delays in account payments as a way of maintaining demand for their goods or services. As the economy entered a new period of growth, these businesses struggled to convince their customers that they should revert back to their normal 30-day credit terms. This lack of proper credit control practices is causing a delay in the recovery of this key business sector, which is essential if the UK economy is to sustain the level of growth necessary to generate jobs for the three and a half million (unofficially!) still unemployed.

As the UK becomes tied ever closer to Europe, our companies will find they are having to compete for orders with our European neighbours. If they are to compete successfully, they will need to match European DSO levels. At the present time German companies collect their debts, on average, 30 days quicker than we do in the UK. As a result they only have to factor 48 days credit into the prices charged for their goods. In the UK we have to factor in 78 days credit. This will result in German goods being marketed at a lower cost than their UK equivalents, and will make them more appealing to cash sensitive consumers.

If UK companies wish to remain competitive with our European neighbours, they need to absorb the additional finance costs associated with their higher debtor days. At present, the only way they can achieve this is by reducing their profit levels; however this will have serious effects on their growth potential and that of the UK economy as a whole.

There is no doubt that poor credit control has a corrosive effect on a company's profit level. The business graveyard is full of companies which failed to collect their debts quickly enough. Even companies that are trading at a profit will eventually meet their demise if they consistently fail to control their debtor base. This problem becomes even more acute during periods of high interest rates, high inflation, or recessionary pressure.

The pie chart in *fig. 11:2*, shows how extended credit cuts into the profit margin of a company. In this example, the company achieves a net profit after tax that equates to 10% of sales. The company pays interest charges of 15% per annum on its overdraft facilities, and its credit terms are 30 days from the date of invoice.

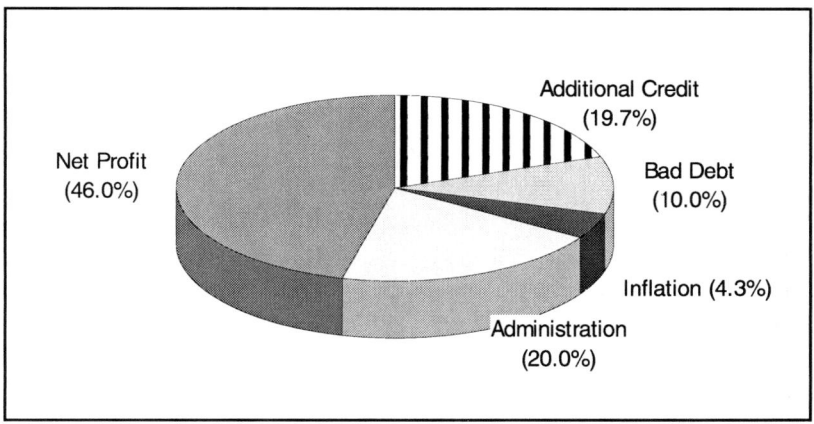

Fig. 11:2 The cost of financing credit and its effect on profit

The costs of financing credit

The costs of overdue debts, that erode a company's profit, fall into four main areas which are as follows:

Financing additional credit

When companies set their price levels, they build in the associated costs of financing their credit sales. If all their customers paid their accounts on time there would not be a problem, but– as you know – this is very rarely the case. The longer it takes a company to collect its debts, the quicker the erosion of its profit. In the example in *fig. 11:2*, we have used the UK average DSO figure of 78 days. As the company has allowed for 30 days credit, its debtors are taking an additional 48 days credit. As this additional credit has not been built into the company's price structure, it will have to be financed separately from the company's profit, or by means of an overdraft.

In the example listed in *fig. 11:2*, the additional cost is calculated as follows: current interest charge, divided by the number of days in the year, multiplied by the extended credit period = costs as a percentage of sales. Multiply the answer by the profit margin to obtain the cost as a percentage of profit. ($15\%/365 \times 48 \times 10 = 19.7\%$)

Bad debt provision

All businesses need to make a provision for bad debts, and the level of provision will depend on three factors: the type of market the business operates in, the quality of its credit control function and the company's policy for calculating its bad debt provision. There are various ways to calculate a bad debt provision, and a company will use whichever method it feels most comfortable with. It should be remembered, however, that if a flat percentage of total debtors is used, you may not be allowed tax relief against the provision. A company should only claim a tax allowance if its bad debt provision is made against specific debtors.

In the example in *fig. 11:2*, the company had a bad debt provision of 1 per cent of sales. The effect of the bad debt provision on profit is calculated as follows: percentage of sales, multiplied by the profit margin, equals the provision as a percentage of profit. ($1\% \times 10 = 10\%$)

Inflation

There will always be a certain level of inflation within the economy, and if the rate is high enough it can seriously affect a company's profit level. It reduces profit by reducing the purchasing power of the money collected from a company's credit sales. Back in 1975, inflation was running at a level of 2% per month. This meant that if a debtor took an additional 60 days credit, by the time his debt was cleared inflation would have reduced the value of the payment by 4%. This is not a problem if the company operates on a high profit margin; however, many retail companies operate their businesses on a policy of high turnover but low profit margin, and only make a net profit of four per cent on their sales. If inflation is running at two per cent per month, these companies only have two months to collect their debts before inflation dissipates their entire profit margin.

When the inflation rate is low this calculation will not have much effect on a company's profits; however, when inflation is running at 25% per annum, as it was under the Labour government in 1975, this equation plays a big part in the profit a company makes.

In the example in *fig. 11:2*, the rate of inflation is calculated at 3.25% per annum. Its effect on profit is calculated as follows: inflation rate, divided by days in the year, times extended credit, equals cost as a percentage of sales, times answer by profit margin, equals cost as a percentage of profit. [(3.25%/365 x 48) x10 = 4.3%]

The cost of administering credit

The longer a debt is overdue, the more it costs to administer. According to surveys carried out by various trade groups, the average cost of administering credit is around two per cent of the gross sales revenue. In the example in *fig. 11:2*, this cost is calculated as follows, cost of administering credit, multiplied by the profit level. (2% x 10 = 20%)

In times of high interest rates, if a company wishes to maintain a healthy profit on its sales it is faced with one of two options: it either has to increase its prices to cover the additional cost of the extended credit, or it has to improve on its credit control performance, thereby reducing its level of borrowing. An increase in prices will usually lead to a reduction in sales, therefore the most beneficial option is to reduce the length of credit it is currently allowing its customers to take. If the company in *fig. 11:2* reduced its DSO figure to 50 days, which is still 20 days beyond terms, it could increase its profit retention by approximately 19%.

Most companies in the UK operate on 30 days credit terms. This means that they only account for the cost of 30 days credit when setting their prices and calculating their profit ratios. As a result, when their debtor days increase above 30, they start to suffer a strain on their cash flow. Some companies, however, are able to absorb the effects of extended credit better than others.

Let us now take a more in-depth look at the effect poor credit control has on a company's profit, and why some companies are better structured to cope with the costs of extended credit.

A company's net profit is basically a derivative of its sales less its cost of sales, other operating expenses, and finally corporation tax. The table in *fig. 11:3*, shows how quickly a company's net profit can be eroded through poor collection procedures.

Months overdue	Interest rate 12.5%	15.0%	17.5%
1	0.01	0.01	0.01
2	0.02	0.03	0.03
3	0.03	0.04	0.04
4	0.04	0.05	0.06
5	0.05	0.06	0.07
6	0.06	0.08	0.09
7	0.07	0.09	0.10
8	0.08	0.10	0.12
9	0.09	0.11	0.13
10	0.10	0.13	0.15

Fig. 11:3 The finance cost of extended credit

Fig. 11:3, shows the cost of financing overdrafts or short term loans at interest rates of 12.5, 15, and 17.5 per cent: and how the costs of financing the extended credit can erode a company's net profit. The quicker a company can collect its trade debts, the lower its costs of financing the debt will be, and therefore the more profit it will retain.

For example, a company that attains a net profit of 4 per cent on sales, needs to collect its debts within 4 months, at an interest charge of 12.5 per cent, if it is to retain any profit. At an interest rate of 15 per cent debts need to be collected in just over three months. At a rate of 17.5 per cent the collection period is reduced to approximately 2.5 months.

The level of extended credit which a company can offer, and still trade at a profit, will be greatly influenced by the mark up the company adds to its production/purchasing costs. The higher the level of net profit a company achieves, the greater the leeway it has when collecting its debts.

In comparison with our previous example, if our company made a net profit of 10 per cent on its sales instead of 4 per cent, at an interest rate of 12.5%, it would have 10 months instead of 4 months to collect its debts while still retaining a profit. At an interest rate of 15 per cent this reduces to 8 months as opposed to 3 months, and at 17.5%, reduces to just under 7 months as opposed to 2.5 months. These figures clearly show the relationship between interest rates and reduced profits, and are one reason why credit control takes on extra importance during a recession, when interest rates are high, and profit margins are low.

Although it is every company's aim to make a profit on the goods or services they sell, this is not the only criterion on which to judge the quality of the sale. It does not necessarily follow that a sale showing no contribution to profits is actually detrimental to the company's trading position. Usually this statement can only be made if a debt goes bad without any money being received from the debtor. Provided the revenue received, less the cost of the extended credit, still covers the variable costs associated with the sale, and contributes something to the company's fixed costs, the company's trading position has still been enhanced.

A company with lower variable costs will be able to absorb a higher level of days sales outstanding, as opposed to a company with higher variable costs. This can be seen more clearly in *fig. 11:4.*

Lowcost Ltd		Highcost Ltd
£		£
20,000	Sales revenue	20,000
(4,000)	Less cost of additional credit	(4,000)
16,000	Revenue generated from sales	16,000
(12,000)	Less variable costs	(17,000)
4,000	Contribution to fixed costs	(1,000)
(10,000)	Fixed costs	(5,000)
(6,000)	Loss	(6,000)

Fig. 11:4 Comparison of companies with differing variable costs

Although both companies made a loss on the sale of £6,000, by virtue of its lower variable costs Lowcost Ltd still made a contribution of £4,000 towards its fixed costs. Therefore its sale has been of benefit to the company, even if it has not been profitable in the true sense of the word. The sale made by Highcost Ltd, has been detrimental to its trading position because it has contributed nothing towards its fixed costs. From this example, and ignoring any other factors, it is quite clear that Highcost Ltd needs to collect its debts more quickly than Lowcost Ltd, if it is to cover its variable costs, and continue to trade.

The effect of credit control on liquidity

When all is said and done, the simple answer to the question: "Why do we need credit control?", is so that a company can retain the level of liquidity it needs to survive. The liquidity of a company is really a measure of how quickly it can turn its current assets into cash. The main composite of current assets for any company will be its trade debtors. Therefore it must follow that the liquidity of a company, is greatly dependant on the ability of that company to convert its debtors into cash.

During the recession we started to see a change in the attitude of British management, regarding the importance of collecting their debts on time. It is imperative that we maintain this momentum even though we have emerged from recession. Growing companies need effective credit control, just as much as those that are struggling to survive. This momentum can be enhanced by making sure companies follow these simple steps listed below, for improved credit control and liquidity.

- ☐ Sales and marketing personnel must be educated on the reasons why the company needs to be paid promptly.
- ☐ The terms of payment should be made very clear to the customer at the point of sale.
- ☐ Chase action should be implemented as soon as a debt becomes overdue.
- ☐ All bad debts begin with the granting of credit facilities. Suitable checks should be made up front on all potential customers. This is standard practice and will not cause offence unless the customer has something to hide.
- ☐ All documentation should show the agreed price and payment terms.
- ☐ Interest to be paid on any overdue accounts should be clearly shown on all paperwork.
- ☐ Follow a proven collection system (see: effective credit control)
- ☐ Make sure all personnel, including sales staff, understand the company's terms and conditions of sale.

12

FACTORING - LENDING ON DEBT

Factoring has existed in one form or another for hundreds of years. However, despite this wealth of experience, and recent levels of growth, the services offered by factors are still poorly promoted and remain a mystery to many of the occupants of company boardrooms across the country. Factoring is denigrated by many as simply the last desperate attempt to salvage an ailing business. But is this a true reflection of one of the fastest growing sectors of the credit market, or are we simply using an outdated stereotype to hide our own ignorance of the services factoring companies offer?

History of factoring

The origin of the factor is lost in the mists of time; however, it is likely that they have existed ever since the development of the crudest form of commerce. They would almost certainly have existed from the twelfth century onwards, when the commerce of Western Europe revolved around the great trade fairs. These fairs would have presented the ideal forum for the early factor. This however is only supposition, as the first recorded mention of a factor does not appear until 1485 in William Caxton's "Lyf of Charles The Great". The term also appears in the works of William Shakespeare (1564-1616).

Factoring

During the middle ages the shipment of commodities from country to country, and communication from one continent to another, was fraught with difficulties. This made life very awkward for manufacturers whose largest markets were quite often overseas. These logistical problems were the main reason why principals needed to trade through factors. The factor would act as an agent for his principal in the warehousing and merchandising of his goods. He would also be responsible for the collection of money owed by his principal's customers. As the role of the factor developed, he would also guarantee the sale of his principal's goods, and on occasion advance payment for those goods before the sale was completed.

As the centuries passed, the role of the factor played an important part in the development of trade between Western Europe and its colonies. They also had an important part to play in the advance of emerging markets, such as the United States, which by the end of the nineteenth century had become an important trading partner for Western Europe. The US relied heavily on Europe to fulfil its textile requirements, and as a result the sheer volume of this business had led to it developing into the most important factoring market in existence.

Between the fifteenth and nineteenth centuries, the role of the factor changed very little. However the turn of the twentieth century saw two fundamental developments that were to change the role of the factor for ever. The first took place in America with a change in attitude of the American Government's trading policy. A sharp move towards protectionism led to new legislation which imposed a punitive tariff on textiles imported into the country.

This resulted in European textiles being priced out of the market, and led to the rapid growth of the US textile industry. As these manufacturers were resident in the US themselves, they no longer required the services of factors to warehouse and merchandise their goods.

The second change came about through the gradual improvement in travel and communications. This more or less eliminated the need for a middle man, and resulted in the role of the factor becoming less important.

Although the full services of the factor were no longer required, all was not lost. Many principals still preferred to trade through their trusted factor, than take the risk of dealing direct with unknown clients. These changes resulted in the streamlining of the services offered by factors, who proceeded to drop the warehousing and merchandising side of their business, concentrating instead on the services of finance and credit.

The streamlining of the services offered by factors also led to changes in the way they operated. They now traded as independent commercial organisations, supplying credit and financial services on a contractual basis of factor and client. The old relationship of factor and principal had gone forever, and the role of the modern day factor was born.

Modern day factoring was introduced into the UK by International Factors Ltd, who started operating in 1960. By the early seventies all the major clearing banks had developed factoring subsidiaries. These subsidiaries are now the principal players in the UK market, which has grown to become the third largest in the world, behind the United States and Italy.

The main services

Although services may vary slightly from company to company, the main services offered by factoring companies are as follows:

Full service factoring

Full service is the most common service offered by factoring companies. It eliminates the need for the participating company to operate a full sales ledger or credit control function, as these are carried out by the factoring company. As a result, this service is very popular with small businesses. Under this arrangement, the factoring company purchases from its client the equity of its debts as each invoice is raised. The factoring company then operates the remaining sales ledger function, and chases for payment as these invoices fall due. As part of the agreement, the factoring company will supply its client with detailed reports of the debts purchased, the level of cash advanced and the level of debts collected.

The full service agreement is usually broken down into one of two types, recourse or non-recourse.

Recourse

With this type of service the client remains liable for any bad debts incurred, along with any debts the factors have been unable to collect. Money advanced against these debts will be recovered by the factor from the client's account.

Non-recourse

Under this agreement the factor will absorb losses incurred by its client, through a debtor's inability to pay. With this type of agreement the factoring company will insist on taking out credit insurance, through a credit insurance company such as Trade Indemnity, or Namur. To obtain this credit insurance, the factor will need to take control of its client's credit sanctioning process. This will take the form of credit checking every new customer its client takes on, and the operating of strict credit limits for these customers.

At this point it is worth noting that it would not be economically viable for companies which have a high level of low-value debts to take out a full service, non-recourse agreement. Even under a non-recourse agreement, the client usually has to absorb the first £500 of any bad debt – although this may vary, depending upon which factoring company is used, and the level of sales-to-customer ratio. As a general rule, the lower the value of each individual sale, the higher the cost of coverage for bad debts.

Invoice discounting

Invoice discounting is provided for clients who wish to maintain their own sales ledger and credit control functions. Under this type of agreement a business receives an advance from the factoring company against its trade debtors, and then acts as an agent for the factors in the collection of its own debts. All money that is collected will then be paid into the factoring company's bank account.

One advantage of this type of factoring is that it is confidential. The participating company's customers do not need to know that it is factoring its debts. This service is popular amongst larger companies, who have developed effective sales ledger and credit control departments. However it is worth noting that this type of factoring is usually subject to a full recourse agreement.

Bulk factoring

Although under this type of agreement a company still has responsibility to collect its own debts, it does have to inform its customers to make payment to the factoring company. Once again, effective in-house credit control and sales ledger functions are a prerequisite to the success of this type of factoring. Bulk factoring is usually taken up by smaller companies that have a high percentage of low-value debts. This type of debtor-to-sales ratio renders a full factoring agreement uneconomic.

The process of factoring

Before we proceed to look at the actual process of factoring, it should be remembered that not all types of businesses are suitable for this type of finance agreement. Businesses that trade in the construction industry, sell goods on a sale or return basis, trade in goods of a perishable nature, trade predominantly with the general public, or deal in areas of a complex nature, are unlikely to secure factoring agreements.

Even if a business fits into an acceptable trade grouping, this in itself does not guarantee that a factoring agreement will be achieved. The spread of a company's debtor base is also an important aspect for factoring companies. They like to see a fairly even spread of sales across the debtor base, with no single customer exceeding more than

25 per cent of the total debtors figure. It is also very important that a business does not offer abnormal or excessive credit terms. No factoring company will advance 80 per cent of a debt that it cannot legally collect for six months.

If after an initial meeting the factoring company considers a business to be a viable candidate, they will then proceed to carry out a business survey. The purpose of this survey is to enable the factor to assess the financial stability of its proposed client. At the same time, it will be making sure that there are no aspects of the company's trading that may affect its title to the book debts. For example, if the company has a previous loan outstanding that is secured by means of a fixed and floating charge on its assets, the factor would not have first call on the book debts if the company ceased to trade.

The company may also be operating a number of contra agreements with its suppliers. This again would invalidate the factoring company's title to these debts. The factor would also view with suspicion any sales to an associate company, or retention of title agreements.

Having assessed the feasibility of the agreement, the factoring company will then move on to the next stage. This incorporates an in-depth review of the debtor list, where the level of sales, average invoice value and number of customers will be assessed. This data is then applied to a standard formula in order to calculate the cost of the service.

Depending on the viability of the business, the factor may look for additional security before proceeding with the agreement. This additional security would probably take the form of one of the following options:

☐ Personal guarantees from the directors/proprietors.
☐ A charge over other assets of the company/business in addition to the book debts.
☐ A charge over the directors'/proprietors' personal assets.

The operation of the agreement

The precise details of the factoring agreement will vary from contract to contract; however, they will not stray too far from the standard mode of operation listed below.

Provided the client is operating a disclosed service, it must ensure that all new invoices carry a notice stating that the debt has been assigned to a factor, and that payment should be made direct to this company. A copy of all invoices raised from the initiation of the agreement must be forwarded to the factor, who will then transfer the client's sales ledger to their own system. After checking and scrutinising the debts, the factor will be able to make the first advance to its client. A typical plan for advanced payments is detailed below.

Sales ledger balance = £200,000
Administration charge = 1.50 % of sales ledger balance.
Initial payment = 80% of total invoice value.
Discount charge = Bank Rate + 3%

The factor credits its client account with 80 per cent of the sales ledger balance, which in this example totals £160,000. At the same time, it applies to its client's account the administration charge of 1.5 per cent, which on a balance of £200,000 equates to £3,000. The client is therefore able to draw cash from his account to the value of £157,000. Interest at 3 per cent above base rate, although this may vary according to individual agreements, is then charged on all borrowing on a daily basis. Interest is recalculated as additional invoices are received by the factor, allowing further drawings; or as payments are received, thereby reducing the level of borrowing.

The debt assigned to the factoring company will then be chased by its own credit controllers. The severity of the chase cycle is usually agreed between the factor and its client. It is important that the client has a level of input at this stage, so that customer goodwill between the client and his customers, and also the factoring company and their client, is maintained. It should be remembered, though, that the factoring company has the final say on how it chases debts assigned to it.

If the required level of collections is not being achieved, it has the legal right to pursue any lawful action it deems necessary to secure payment.

The operation of the client's account will be monitored by the client/account manager. The job of the client manager is to foster a good working relationship between the factor and its client. He will also monitor the level of collections being achieved from the client's debtors. The level of collections is monitored for two reasons: first, to make sure that the credit controllers are working at their optimum level; and then, to make sure that the level of queries being generated on the accounts is not excessive.

The client manager will also be vigilant against the possibility of fraud by the client. Fraud is most commonly perpetrated, either by the factoring of fictitious debts, or through the collecting and banking of payments by the client which should go to the factor. To prevent fraud, the factor will verify the invoices supplied to it on a continuous basis. This verification will take the form of making sure there are not any duplicated, or postdated invoices being passed across by the client.

The financial cost of factoring

There are basically three types of charge raised by a factoring company:

Administration charge

The administration charge is also known as the service or commission charge. This charge is calculated as an agreed percentage of the total debtors figure. The level of this charge will very depending on the factor used and the type of service rendered. The expected sales volume, number of debtors and average value of debt will also have an effect on the eventual amount charged. For full service, non- recourse arrangements it will also cover the cost of bad debt protection.

The purpose of the administration charge is to cover the costs incurred by the Factor, while carrying out its clients sales ledger and credit control activities. It should be remembered that even under an

Implementing Successful Credit Control

invoice discounting agreement, where the client controls its own sales ledger and credit control functions, there will still be a small admin charge. This charge is raised to cover the cost of monitoring the account. Administration charges usually vary from 0.5 to 4 per cent of the gross value of each invoice.

Discount charge

The discount charge is just another name for the amount of interest levied on the funds advanced to the client. This charge is usually between 2 and 3 per cent above base rate, and is normally around the same level as Bank overdraft rates. As explained earlier in this chapter it is calculated on a daily basis.

Re-factoring charge

On occasion a factor may make an additional administration charge, known as a re-factoring charge. This fee, usually one per cent, is charged on debts over 90 days old that are proving difficult and time consuming to collect. However it should be noted that this charge does not cover costs incurred by the factoring company as a result of having to take legal action to recover a debt. Costs for legal action are passed onto the client as a separate charge.

Cost comparison

Before we proceed to look at the cost comparisons listed below, I should state that it would be difficult to use these comparisons on their own to make a decision as to which service to use. Other factors such as the adverse effect factoring may have on your business; any reduction in the level of bad debts your company may benefit from through using a factoring company; the effect on the growth potential of your business, and whether you can secure your required level of financing from a bank, all need to be considered before a decision is made.

160

In the following examples I have also chosen to use the same level of interest for loans from the bank and the factoring company, which are quite often parallel. However, it should be remembered that each factoring arrangement is negotiated on its own merits, and rates can vary, depending on which factor you use.

Fig. 12:1 shows a comparison between factoring & in-house collection costs for Needaloan Ltd, who have annual sales of £30,000,000 and a DSO level of 78 days, which is equivalent to the national average. Staff costs for Needaloan are calculated at salary plus 50 per cent. The overdraft requirements are governed by the need to finance its DSO level. At present, Needaloan Ltd employs five credit controllers and five sales ledger clerks.

Needaloan Ltd: Collection Costs

Collection costs	In-house	Full Service	Invoice Discounting
	£	£	£
Credit controllers	150,000	22,500	150,000
Sales ledger clerks	100,000	18,500	100,000
Overdraft (6,410,000 @10%)	641,000	–	–
Discount charge (6,410,000 @10%)	–	641,000	641,000
Service charge (30,000,000 @2%)	–	600,000	–
Service charge (30,000,000 @0.5%)	–	–	150,000
Total costs	891,000	1,282,000	1,041,000

Fig. 12:1 Comparison of collection costs for Needaloan Ltd

It should be remembered that, even when looking at a full service agreement, Needaloan will still need to employ one credit controller and one sales ledger clerk.

Justbegun Ltd (*fig 12:2*) has been trading for two years, has annual sales of £1,000,000 and a DSO level of 95 days. Once again, staff costs are calculated at salary plus 50 per cent. Their overdraft requirements are governed by their need to finance their DSO level. Justbegun Ltd employs one credit controller and one sales ledger clerk.

Justbegun Ltd: Collection Costs			
Collection costs	In-house	Full Service	Bulk Factoring
	£	£	£
Credit controllers	24,000	–	24,000
Sales ledger clerks	18,000	18,000	18,000
Overdraft (260,270 @10%)	26,027	–	–
Discount charge (260,270 @10%)	–	26,027	26,027
Service charge (1,000,000 @2%)	–	20,000	–
Service charge (1,000,000 @0.5%)	–	–	5,000
Total costs	68,027	64,027	73,027

Fig. 12:2 Comparison of collection costs for Justbegun Ltd

It appears from the results listed in *figs. 12:1* and *12:2* that Needaloan Ltd would not gain any benefit, costwise, by factoring its debts, while Justbegun Ltd would achieve a small saving by using a full factoring service. However, it is only fair to assume that when a factoring company takes on a full service agreement it will be able to reduce its client's DSO levels. With this in mind, let's take another look at Needaloan Ltd.

Needaloan Ltd: Revised Collection Costs			
Collection costs	In-house	Full Service	Invoice Discounting
	£	£	£
Credit controllers	150,000	22,500	150,000
Sales ledger clerks	100,000	18,500	100,000
Overdraft (6,410,000 @10%)	641,000	–	–
Discount charge (4,520,000 @10%)	–	452,000	–
Discount charge (6,410,000 @10%)	–	–	641,000
Service charge (30,000,000 @2%)	–	600,000	–
Service charge (30,000,000 @0.5%)	–	–	150,000
Total costs	891,000	1,093,000	1,041,000

Fig. 12:3 Revised collection costs for Needaloan Ltd

In this scenario, we find that the factoring company has managed to reduce Needaloan's DSO level to 55 days. This in turn has resulted in their borrowing requirements being reduced.

The results listed in *Fig. 12:3* clearly show that it is still more cost-effective for Needaloan Ltd to collect its debts in-house. If they improved the quality of their own credit control function to rank alongside that of the factoring company, they could reduce their collection costs by a further £189,000. This saving could then be reinvested in the company, thereby increasing growth potential.

As would be expected, the impact made by the factor on the debts of Justbegun Ltd, is even more dramatic. The DSO level has now reduced from 95 to 65 days. Once again this has led to reduced borrowing costs, with the following results:

Justbegun Ltd: Revised Collection Costs

Collection costs	In-house	Full Service	Bulk Factoring
	£	£	£
Credit controllers	24,000	–	24,000
Sales ledger clerks	18,000	18,000	18,000
Overdraft (260,270 @10%)	26,027	–	–
Discount charge (178080 @10%)	–	17,808	–
Discount charge (260,270 @10%)	–	–	26,027
Service charge (1,000,000 @2%)	–	20,000	–
Service charge (1,000,000 @0.5%)	–	–	5,000
Total costs	68,027	55,808	73,027

Fig. 12:4 Revised collection results for Justbegun Ltd

The results in *fig. 12:4* show an increase in the benefits Justbegun Ltd receives from having a full service factoring agreement. It is unlikely at this stage in its development that, left to its own devices, Justbegun ltd could achieve the same level of collection success in-house.

The law of factoring

Because the law of factoring is so complex and ill-defined, proper legal advice should be sought if you do not fully understand the legalities of a factoring agreement. The difficulty in clarification of factoring law probably arises from the way factoring has developed from its early forms. As stated earlier in this chapter, factoring was imported into this country from the United States and little thought was given to the differences in the laws governing the two countries. In the United States they have a uniform commercial code which clarifies the law of factoring; unfortunately, in the UK there is no such clarification.

To enable a factor to trade freely, it needs to know that it has legal title to the debts it is purchasing. This, however, is not as easily achieved as you may at first think.

According to the law, debts are a type of intangible property, in which physical possession cannot exist. Therefore, the client can not sell a debt to the factor in the same way he would sell him his watch. The factoring agreement actually transfers to the factor the benefit (i.e., payment) that its client is legally contracted to receive from his customer.

To satisfy the Law of Property Act 1925, section 136, the transfer of equity must be made in such a way as to satisfy the following requirements:

☐ The transfer must be absolute.(i.e., the full debt must be transferred.)
☐ The agreement between the client and the factor must be in writing, and signed by the client.
☐ The receiver of the goods or services must be notified in writing of the transfer.

As it is only the equity, and not the actual debt, that is transferred to the factor, the title to the debt from an enforcement point of view remains jointly between the factor and his client. This means that if the factor wished to proceed with legal action to recover a debt the action would have to be instigated jointly by the factor and its client.

This could prove somewhat difficult, especially if the client did not wish to proceed with legal action against one of his customers. To overcome this situation, factoring agreements always contain a clause assigning to the factor an irrevocable power of attorney. This allows the factor to proceed with any recovery action through the courts in their name only.

Conclusions

Factors definitely have a role to play within the world of commerce. There is no doubt that small businesses and the economy as a whole can benefit greatly from the services they offer, as it is this very sector that forms the bedrock of economic growth within this country. As such, its success is of paramount importance if we are to create the level of jobs necessary to move back towards full employment. Unfortunately, this sector has a bad record of credit control and cash flow management, and it is here that factors can best wield their influence to help create a thriving economy. Small businesses need the discipline of good credit management and sustainable growth levels. These disciplines are the cornerstone of effective factoring.

When we move into the medium-to-large business sectors, the picture changes. I do not believe factors have much to offer bigger companies. The most cost effective way for these businesses to operate, is for them to develop their own, effective, in-house collection systems. Unlike companies in either the small or large sectors, medium-size businesses would definitely suffer from the tarnished image of factoring.

Factoring companies are not superhuman. They do not possess magical powers that help them to collect debts. They have simply developed effective collection techniques, which they administer in a very professional manner. I believe my credit control department is as effective at collecting debts as any factoring company. If the company I work for can achieve this, in a market not renowned for good credit practices, then anyone can. All you need is the right discipline to be exerted from the top and a professional attitude towards the collection of overdue debts.

The advantages of factoring:

☐ Factoring provides businesses with finance for working capital requirements. This in turn can help reduce the effects of poor cash flow, which is one of the main causes of company insolvency.

☐ Many small businesses do not have the level of security demanded by the major banks, to meet the level of borrowing required. The banks will usually only lend 50 per cent of the value of book debts. A factoring company will lend up to 80 per cent – sometimes more.

☐ A factoring company's security against its loan usually lies totally in the book debts of its client. Therefore, unlike banks, it is not overly concerned in overall balance sheet strength. Any asset the company has, with the exception of trade debtors, can be used alongside factoring to secure other financing.

☐ Because funds from Factoring companies are provided as a percentage of sales, the risk of overtrading is reduced.

☐ Smaller companies can be relieved of their sales ledger and credit control responsibilities, thereby allowing the company to devote all its time to the development of the business.

☐ Factoring forces companies to adopt proper and effective credit control procedures.

The disadvantages of factoring:

☐ As the level of finance advanced by the factoring company is tied to approximately 75 per cent of sales, it is difficult for the participating company to finance any significant level of growth, without obtaining other forms of financing.

☐ The costs of obtaining finance through a factoring agreement are usually higher than the costs of a normal overdraft facility. This reflects the increased level of risk taken by factoring companies.

☐ Under full service, non-recourse agreements, companies experience a loss of control over their sales ledger and credit control functions. It is not unusual for companies to find themselves being told which customers they can sell to on credit, and at what level. This action can result in adverse pressure being placed on the growth potential of the company.

☐ Although factoring in the UK still has an image of desperation, the last desperate act of a dying company, it has been shown here that this is not always the case. Some companies factor their debts because they see it as the most efficient way for them to run their business. However, these are usually small businesses – medium-size companies could give the impression of financial weakness if they enter into a factoring agreement.

☐ It should be remembered that factoring is not a panacea. It will not be of much help to companies that operate in an industry that suffers from notoriously slow paying customers, or high levels of bad debts.

GLOSSARY OF COMMON TERMS AND PHRASES

Acid Test Ratio:

    A measure of a company's ability to meet its short term obligations. Calculated as: Current Assets less Stock and Work In Progress, divided by Current Liabilities. This ratio is also known as the quick ratio.

Bad Debt:

    Money owed to a company which it is unable to collect.

Balance Sheet:

    A statement listing the assets and liabilities of a company at a given time. It will always be calculated at a company's year end, and forms part of its annual accounts.

Bank Overdraft:

    This is usually an agreed amount, borrowed from the bank on a continuous basis, to fund the day-to-day trading activities of the company. Interest rates on overdrafts are usually charged at approximately 3 per cent above base rate.

Bankruptcy:

    A person is declared bankrupt by the courts, either at his own request, or through action taken by a creditor.

Cash Flow:
The level of money required by a company to meet the costs of its normal trading activity.

Credit:
The ability to obtain goods, services, or finance on the promise of repayment within the stated credit period.

Credit Controller:
A person who is responsible for the recovery of money owed to the company by its debtors.

Credit Manager:
Manager responsible for the control of a company's credit sanctioning process, and the developing and overseeing of its collection procedures.

Current Assets:
Assets that can be turned into cash within a 12 month period.

Current Liabilities:
Liabilities due for payment within a 12 month period.

Default Summons:
Summons issued in the County Court by a creditor, to recover money owed to it by its debtor.

Debtor:
A customer who purchases goods or services on credit.

DSO:
Abbreviation for Days Sales Outstanding. This is a calculation of the length of time it is taking a company to collect payment from its customers.

Financial Controller:

The person in charge of the day-to-day running of the accounts function.

Financial Director:

Director who sits on the board of a limited company, and is responsible for all the company's financial affairs.

Fixed Assets:

Assets such as buildings, machinery and other equipment. These assets usually have a relatively long life, and are used to facilitate the production of goods or services which make up the basis of a company's trading activity.

Gross Profit:

Sales, less the costs of sales.

Insolvency:

A company or individual is deemed to be insolvent if it can no longer finance its debts. Technically, this occurs when current liabilities exceed current assets. At this stage a company is deemed to have a negative working capital.

Limited Liability:

The liability of shareholders in private or public limited companies, which is restricted to the level of their shareholding. If their shareholding is fully paid, then they have no other liability for a company's debts. If their shares are part-paid, they are liable for the company's debts up to the amount of their unpaid shareholding.

Liquidation:

The process of winding up a limited company, usually because of insolvency. This can occur as a result of a court order (see chapter 8), or voluntarily after a meeting of the company's shareholders.

Liquidity:

The excess of current assets over current liabilities.

Net Worth:

An indication of the financial strength of a company, calculated as: Total Assets less Total Liabilities. This calculation is often carried out after deducting intangible assets, such as goodwill.

Plaintiff:

The party instigating legal action against another, for the recovery of its debts.

Profit Margin:

Margin of profit made on each item sold. Calculated as: pre tax profit/loss, as percentage of turnover.

Registered Office:

The official address of a limited company, for legal matters.

Undischarged Bankrupt:

A bankrupt who has not been discharged from his responsibilities to his creditors.

Working Capital:

Indicates the ability of a company to finance its day-to-day trading activities. Calculated as: Current Assets less Current Liabilities. A more exact measure of Working Capital is described under Acid Test Ratio.

BIBLIOGRAPHY

Adams J & Brownsword R: *Understanding Law*: Fountain Press 1992
Armstrong M: *How To Be An Even Better Manager*: Kogan Page 1994
Barry M A: *Debt Recovery In The County Courts*: Croner Publishing Ltd 1992
Salinger F R: *Factoring*: Tolley Publishing Co. Ltd 1984
Spencer J C: *Getting Paid*: Management Books 2000 Ltd 1991
Encyclopedia America: Volume 10
Encyclopedia Britannica: Volume 9
The New Encyclopedia Britannica: Volume 4
Factoring In The UK: B C R Industry Report.

INDEX

Grievance call, 39

Hanging up (of telephone), 56
Harassment, 26, 83
High Court, 104, 110-111

Inflation, allowing for, 147
Influencing factors, 80
Insolvency Act 1986, 34
Institute of Credit Management, 23
Interpleader Summons, 112
Invoice discounting, 155
Invoices,
    cash-managing, 36
Issuing legal proceedings, 106, 111

Judgement debt, enforcement, 111

Law of Property Act 1925, 164
Legal action, 26, 85, 103
    proceeding with, 104
    issuing, 106
Letters, 56
Limited liability, 29
Liquidation, 115
Liquidity, 123, 150
    ratio, 123

Management style, 31
Maslow, Abraham, 42
Mass production, 17
Motivation, 42
    of Credit Control staff, 31

Need to belong, 32
Negotiation
    agreeing instalments, 76
    withdrawal from, 76
Non-recourse factoring, 155

Oral examination, 114
Overdraft, 21
    securing of, 115

Payment
    discount, 84
    negotiation of, 73
    options, 55

penalty, 84
Phoenix companies, 116
Post, cheque is in the, 69
Power phase, 65
Proceedings, issuing, 111
Profitability, 127
    ratio, 127

Question,
    leading, 48-9
    opening, 48-9
    probe, 48-50
Quick ratio (see also acid test), 125

Ratio analysis, 122
Recession, 15, 21-22, 35
Recourse factoring, 155
Re-factoring, 160
References,
    bank, 120
    trade, 119
Reversing arguments, 52, 70
Revolving credit, 14

Sales department, 18, 41
Sales staff, 20
Self-belief, importance of, 45
Selye, Professor Hans, 130
Sheriff's office, 111
Slow payment, reasons for, 35
Small businesses., problems with, 29
Solicitor, 89
    cost of using, 101
    choosing, 101
Status reports, 121
Statutory Demand, 116
Stress, 129
    causes of, 132
    effects of, 131
    effects on Credit Control, 136
    environmental causes, 134
    symptoms of, 130, 136
    ways of reducing, 138
Summary Judgement, 104, 108, 111
Summons, 106